the
fresh20

20-Ingredient Meal Plans for Health and Happiness 5 Nights a Week

MELISSA LANZ

WILLIAM MORROW
An Imprint of HarperCollinsPublishers

 For information address HarperCollins Publishers, 195 Broadway, New York, NY 10007.

HarperCollins books may be purchased for educational, business, or sales promotional use. For information, please e-mail the Special Markets Department at SPsales@harpercollins. com.

FIRST EDITION

Designed by Shannon Plunkett

Library of Congress Cataloging-in-Publication Data has been applied for.

ISBN 978-0-06-220098-3

15 16 17 SCP 10 9 8 7 6 5

For my mother, Eileen.
You are missed at the table.

CONTENTS

The Fresh 20 *is a meal-planning service that uses only twenty seasonal ingredients per week to cook five weeknight dinners. The mission is to improve family food culture by focusing on whole foods the entire family can enjoy.*

The Fresh 20 can help you:

- Eat well
- Eliminate processed foods
- Control portions
- Save time
- Save money
- Increase quality family time
- Reduce waste
- Cook with ease

FUJI APPLES
1.98 LB
1.98 LB
1.98 LB

I was raised on Swanson's TV dinners and a steady stream of meat and potatoes. I started cooking at an early age from the pages of *The Good Housekeeping Illustrated Cookbook* and never looked back. Over the years, I became the go-to cook for my family. Yet, although I liked to eat, I was not always a mindful eater. I often ate for comfort and sometimes out of boredom. My jeans have seen everything from a size 4 to a size 14.

It took years to overcome my initial family food culture of processed foods and takeout and find my way to the cooking I enjoy today. These days, I eat with much more consciousness and a deliberate eye toward health.

The Fresh 20 grew out of my own journey. I did not always eat fresh, but now I make the connection between what I eat and how I feel. It's important to start early and institute a healthy family food culture your children can draw on for the rest of their lives. I didn't have that and it took me years to find, so I wanted my kids to get a head start. The challenge came when I couldn't find an easy way to put a healthy and tasty dinner on the table every night. So I worked out a plan that helps me do just that. I call it The Fresh 20.

If I can go from being a frozen burrito addict to maintaining a fresh kitchen, I promise that you can too!

I hope that my efforts will inspire you on your own road to an enriched and healthy family food culture.

To your wild kitchen success,

Melissa

how to use THE FRESH 20

The Fresh 20 started as an online Web service focused on a whole-foods lifestyle. I launched the website in 2010, leaving a sixty-hour-a-week corporate job behind to create something useful and meaningful for my young family. The meal plans in this book are based on The Fresh 20 philosophy and are designed to get you to the family dinner table with health and happiness.

The book shows you **how to plan ahead and cook five dinners a week** using only 20 fresh, seasonal ingredients. The meal plans focus on weeknight meals for busy families who want to eat well and enjoy dinnertime. The meals were created with nutrition, taste, and ease in mind. Every recipe offers a healthy, tasty alternative to processed, take-out, and packaged food.

The Fresh 20 mission is about **buying less and making more.** It's about loading your dinner table with delicious preservative-free food. It's about planning and cooking in a way that eliminates last-minute stress and overly complicated preparation from an already overloaded life. It's about looking around your dinner table and being happy to be exactly where you are, surrounded by your family, digging into a meal that nurtures body, soul, and the connections among people.

The Fresh 20 recipes are delicious, but they do not require an hour in the grocery store, multiple stops for ingredients, or a shopping list with eighty items. By planning well, you save time, avoid waste, and **stop throwing money down the drain**. The meal plans were carefully created to use everything you purchase. Instead of grabbing five unrelated recipes and spitting out a shopping list, The Fresh 20 helps you plan a week of meals that mix and match a short list of seasonal ingredients to create five well-planned, balanced dinners. One day's roast becomes another evening's soup or pasta. It's dinner as usual without the same old, same old.

Also included in the book are sidebars that go beyond the recipes, with notes on Do It

Yourself condiments and pantry items, fresh ideas to keep you motivated, and family profiles of The Fresh 20 community of chefs, friends, and subscribers. Take a minute to look over The Fresh 20 Pantry Essentials (page xix) and the list of tools in The Fresh 20 Kitchen Tools (page xxvii). These are basics I have on hand to help make dinner with ease.

This book may not solve all your family weeknight issues—I can't turn your spouse's cell phone off or get them to turn off the playoff game—but it is committed to getting the family dinner back on track.

Shop

Grocery shopping is an important element of The Fresh 20. Planning ahead can reduce stress, but it takes time. The Fresh 20 saves time. Each week's shopping list contains 20 items. I want you to use the freshest ingredients you can get your hands on. Well-cared-for local ingredients will always taste better than produce that has made a long journey, but I believe it is better to cook with something fresh even if it's not immediately local. Organic food is mostly regional, because organic produce does not keep as long as sprayed fruits and vegetables. Eating in season is also less expensive.

The shopping lists in this book are categorized and easy to follow so even noncooks and kids can help with the grocery tasks. When possible, shopping at a farmers' market on the weekends can be a productive and memory-making family affair, and it will often save you money.

At the Grocery Store

Stick to the plan—it's easy to get sidetracked by shiny items in the store. Buy only the items on your list and satisfy any junk food cravings at home with a healthy snack.

Stay on the perimeter of the store where the fresh food is located. In general, the middle aisles are laden with processed foods. Keep it fresh by walking on the outside.

Buying Organic

The organic label can be confusing. Is it worth it? Is it healthier?

I buy certain items organic because I want to eliminate as many pesticides and chemicals in my food as possible. Check the dirty dozen list at **www.ewg.org** for the produce with the highest levels of pesticides and make your own decisions about what in your cart is organic. In my house, organic strawberries are a must! I buy organic dairy, canned tomatoes, and tomato paste whenever possible.

Prep

Chop a few vegetables, snip some herbs, wash some fruit—taking some time before the week starts to prep your meals makes it a lot easier when dinnertime comes. The prep guides included in each section outline what can be made ahead each week.

Prep Guide Basics

You will find directions for many of our most frequent prep-ahead items throughout the book.

The Fresh 20 Spice Blend, page xxii

Grains: Brown Rice, Quinoa, Couscous, page xvii

Pantry Dressings, pages 26–27

Beans, page 39

Cook

Some recipe basics:

Meals serve 4 adults (or 2 adults and 2 kids, with leftovers for a lunch).

Eggs: I use large organic.

Yogurt: I recommend low-fat plain Greek.

Milk: Use 2% unless otherwise noted.

Special Diets: Gluten-free, dairy-free, and vegetarian recipes are indicated with an icon. GF DF V

Leftovers

Nothing, including your time, goes to waste with The Fresh 20. If recipes on Monday and Wednesday both call for roasted chicken, Monday's recipe calls for cooking extra chicken to be stored and then reheated for Wednesday's meal. When an ingredient is used in this way, I provide specific instructions in Leftover Notes for how to store and reheat.

Tips for Success

- Read through each recipe before starting.
- *Mise en place* (literally, "put in place")—get all the ingredients ready before starting to cook. Ingredients lists are given with the ingredients prepped/cut/etc.; directions assume all the ingredients are ready. Refer back to Prep Ahead sections as appropriate.
- Taste as you go—the idea is that when we cook, we control the outcome and the healthfulness. Trust your palate, listen to your body.
- Be creative! It's about you and your family. You can follow the meal plans and recipes exactly, but they can also serve as simple guidelines. If you come up with a great adaptation, let me know—I'd love to see what is cooking in your kitchen!

A Note About Nutritional Data and Counting Calories

I feel it is far more important to concentrate on common-sense eating than it is to count every calorie. I hear from many The Fresh 20 subscribers about their weight-loss goals and their need for specific nutrition information. We need to use all the tools available to us to make healthy decisions about food intake, and if calorie, fat, and sugar data help you stay on track, you'll find no objection from me. But you will not find nutritional data here—my intention is to get you started in the kitchen with fresh ingredients. Nutritional analyses can never replace learning sustainable, healthy eating habits and visual portion control. However, for anyone on a restricted diet, all the nutritional data for every meal can be found at www.thefresh20.com/cookbook.

grains

Brown Rice

1 teaspoon olive oil

1 cup long-grain brown rice

2 cups low-sodium chicken or vegetable broth or water

½ teaspoon kosher salt (only if using water)

1. Heat the oil in a small stockpot on medium heat.

2. Add the dry rice and coat with the oil.

3. Let the rice toast for 2 to 3 minutes.

4. Stir in the broth or water and salt.

5. Cover and reduce the heat to low and simmer for 30 minutes.

6. Remove from the heat and let steam for 5 minutes before lifting the lid.

Yield: 1 cup dry makes 2 cups prepared

Quinoa

1 teaspoon olive oil

1 cup quinoa

2 cups low-sodium chicken or vegetable broth or water

¼ teaspoon kosher salt (only if using water)

1. Heat the oil in a small stockpot on medium heat.

2. Add the dry quinoa and coat with the oil.

3. Let the quinoa toast for 2 to 3 minutes.

4. Stir in the broth or water and salt.

5. Cover and reduce the heat to low and simmer for 25 minutes.

Yield: 1 cup dry quinoa makes 2.5 cups prepared

Couscous

1½ cups low-sodium chicken or vegetable broth or water

1 cup couscous

1 teaspoon olive oil

⅛ teaspoon kosher salt (only if using water)

1. In a small stockpot, bring the broth or water to a boil.

2. Add the oil and if using water, salt.

3. Stir in the dry couscous, cover, remove from the heat, and let stand for 5 minutes.

4. Stir to fluff up and serve.

Yield: 1 cup dry couscous makes 3 cups prepared

My pantry is the heart of my kitchen. I search its shelves when I'm looking for inspiration or a last-minute dinner fix. At the center of The Fresh 20 is the concept that even with limited resources (little time, ingredients, tools, patience, even sanity), you can make delicious and healthy meals. But this means the resources you do have on hand need to be true workhorses of the kitchen. I have handpicked these pantry items with this in mind. These few items make it possible to create The Fresh 20 meals with minimal effort.

I have two rules regarding the pantry: 1) keep it simple and 2) invest in good-quality ingredients. Here is a shopping list for stocking your The Fresh 20 Pantry. These items will soon become your most trusted kitchen companions.

Note: *This list is not exhaustive by any means. It is a basic pantry of essential items. In each week's shopping list, I remind you which pantry items you'll need, so you can stock up if you are running low. Check the Resources at www.thefresh20.com for a list of my favorites and where to buy them.*

- **Olive Oil**

  Olive oil is a kitchen foundation. It is an excellent replacement for butter in healthy cooking. I prefer brands with a nice balance between fruity and peppery. Some olive oils are heavier on the tongue and can weigh down food. The range of oils available is huge, so take the opportunity to sample oils at stores and even friends' houses and figure out the ones you like. Your taste is more important than any labels. Because I use olive oil in almost every meal, I save money by buying it in large tins at an Italian market. I use olive oil for sautéing, in dressings, for pasta or rice, and for drizzling over anything roasted.

- **Grapeseed Oil**

  Grapeseed oil has a milder flavor than most vegetable oils and a high smoke point, which makes it great for searing, frying, and grilling. Look for bottles that say "cold pressed" on the label. Like any cooking oil, grapeseed oil is best stored out of direct sunlight.

Balsamic Vinegar

Authentic balsamic vinegar from Italy's Modena and Reggio Emilia regions might be too expensive for simple weeknight meals. In Italy, aged balsamic vinegar is used sparingly, as a condiment. But there are plenty of less-expensive balsamic-style vinegars in the grocery store that can lend zip to stir-fried dishes, marinades, and salad dressings. Look for aged natural vinegar with no color additives or sweeteners.

Vinegar

I use white wine vinegar to make salad dressings, marinades, and quick pickles. Look for an all-natural vinegar. Rice vinegar is lovely as well and slightly less acidic. Many people prefer the fruitiness of apple cider vinegar. In most cases, these vinegars can be used interchangeably in The Fresh 20 recipes. Taste and decide which one should be in your pantry based on your family's preference.

Chicken or Vegetable Broth

Good broth is one of the secrets to healthy cooking. Broth often eliminates the need for additional fat, replacing oil or butter, for example, when softening onions. It can be used instead of oil in many pasta or rice dishes. Make your own and freeze it in small quantities for quick use, or buy a high-quality organic, low-sodium variety. I generally keep both chicken and vegetable broth on hand, as they have distinctive flavors. **For DIY Chicken Broth, see page 240.**

Garlic

Garlic is the only perishable on my pantry list, but I use it often enough that it never goes bad. Garlic is freshest from June to September. Buying peeled garlic is a time saver, but it's simple to crush the cloves with a chef's knife to release them from their papery skins. Or let the kids use a rubber garlic roller to shed the garlic skin with a little magic. If the garlic seems dried out, leave it at the store; it is on the downhill side of flavor and can be bitter. Bad garlic can ruin a meal.

Herbes de Provence

Some consider this pantry item exotic, but I stand behind its utility. This unique blend of aromatics gives a floral note to meats, fish, and poultry. The mix of dried herbs, commonly found in southern France, includes basil, fennel, thyme, and lavender. It's perfect for roasted chicken and in side dishes like grains or legumes. Specialty stores carry herbes de Provence if your local market hasn't caught on yet.

Honey and Maple Syrup

The health questions surrounding sugar are never ending, but I believe everything should be consumed in moderation, and I buy sugar in its most natural form. Honey comes straight from the hive, which gives it whole-food status. For vegans, maple syrup is a satisfying unprocessed alternative sweetener. Always purchase 100 percent pure maple syrup and skip brands blended with cane sugar water. I use organic Grade A amber, but it can be expensive. Your sugar selection comes down to personal preference for a recipe.

Soy Sauce

I love soy sauce, mostly used in stir-fries and marinades, for its ability to serve in many roles while keeping its own identity. Its salty taste imparts a rich, dense flavor to many dishes. Those on gluten-free diets should look for tamari instead of soy sauce; it contains no wheat, but the flavor profile is very similar. I prefer reduced-sodium soy sauce.

Dried Oregano

If I could choose only one dried herb, it would be oregano for its versatility. Traditionally oregano pairs well with Italian and Greek cuisine. I like it in beans, soups, and salads. Even though dried, oregano should still look vibrant, not brown and dull.

a fresh idea:

THE FRESH 20 SPICE BLEND

This blend goes with practically anything. Keep some on hand for grilling. It's also great for rubbing on vegetables before roasting and to season salads.

MAKES A GENEROUS 2 TABLESPOONS

1 Tablespoon ground cumin
1½ teaspoons black pepper
1½ teaspoons kosher salt
½ teaspoon sweet paprika
¼ teaspoon cayenne pepper

Kosher Salt

If you are still using iodized table salt, my heart goes out to your food: it's suffering. Table salt has an acidic flavor. The granules are smaller and more of it is required to bring out any real flavor. Good kosher salt is coarse and has no additives. Try the Diamond brand. If you prefer sea salt, I understand—I like it too and use different types on weekends, when I have time to slow-cook dishes. If you do substitute sea salt, you will need to adjust the salt quantities in the recipes: because of its density, less sea salt is required.

Black Pepper

Many dishes are improved with a dash of black pepper. It stimulates the palate and adds a hint of spiciness. Buy whole peppercorns to grind fresh with a pepper mill at mealtime. Avoid ground black pepper, which often includes additives and has already lost some of its potency. My preference leans toward Tellicherry peppercorns, but any fresh whole peppercorns will produce flavorful results.

Ground Cumin

Earthy and slightly bitter, cumin is my all-purpose powder. In my kitchen, it is known as the global spice, invoking flavors from the Mediterranean to Mexico and even making its way into American barbecue. Good for marinades, spice rubs, and sauces.

Paprika

Made from ground dried chile peppers, paprika is a fragrant, sweet spice that is surprisingly versatile but often overlooked. It adds vibrant color to dishes and releases a lot of flavor when slowly heated. There are three types of paprika: sweet, hot, and smoked. The Fresh 20 recipes use sweet Hungarian paprika. Most of the paprika in the grocery store has little scent or flavor, so I recommend purchasing it online; see Resources, page 263.

Cayenne Pepper

I use cayenne pepper to add just the right amount of heat to certain recipes. Don't confuse cayenne pepper with chili powder, which is a blend of several spices and has a smoky flavor profile. Cayenne pepper varies drastically in heat and quality. Choose a brand that doesn't use additives.

Whole Wheat Pasta

My rule for pasta is simple: the fewer ingredients in the dish, the higher quality the pasta. Whole wheat or whole-grain flour produces dense noodles with an earthy scent. I choose whole wheat pasta because the flour is closest to its natural form—it hasn't been stripped of nutrients as white flour has. There are many brands available in most supermarkets.

Brown Rice

If there is one element I would change about our family food cultures, it is our dependency on white rice. I use brown rice because the germ, which contains most of the nutrients, is still intact (it has been removed from white rice). If your family is hesitant to make the switch, try a half-and-half blend to start. And check out the basic brown rice recipe on page xvii—it's so good you won't miss the white variety.

Whole Wheat Flour

I had no idea flour had real taste until I discovered whole wheat flour, which is nutty, dense, and wholesome. Avoid bleached or chemically processed varieties—buy stone-ground or milled flour. Whole wheat pastry flour is less dense than regular whole wheat flour. If you are new to whole wheat, look for whole wheat white flour, which is similar to regular white flour but includes the germ. Flour absorbs odors, so the best way to store it is in an airtight container in the refrigerator.

Dijon Mustard

Dijon is the middle man of spices, bringing together a wide range of flavors. It also helps bind olive oil and vinegar in dressings and marinades. It adds flavor to meats. And it is a good alternative to mayonnaise in sandwiches. A little goes a long way.

Tomato Paste

This tomato concentrate adds depth to soups, sauces, and even dressings. I buy mine in tubes so I can use a tablespoon at a time without wasting a can, and I always buy organic. Look for brands with no added salt.

tomato
PASTE

1 TEASPOON
1 TABLESPOON
1/2 TEASPOON

THE FRESH 20 KITCHEN *tools*

Food doesn't taste better just because someone prepared it using a three-hundred-dollar appliance. The best food I've ever eaten has been prepared in simple home kitchens with very few utensils. I spent my college days cooking everything from coq au vin to brownies using only two tools: a dull chef's knife and a wooden spoon. That being said, as the years passed, cooking became a more pleasant endeavor with the addition of a few basic utensils, and it is easier to get weeknight dinners on the table with more than just a wooden spoon and a knife. Here I share with you my list of lifesavers for cooking with ease and grace. And by ease and grace, I mean cutting up a tomato without having to put your full body weight into the task.

BASICS

- **Measuring Spoons and Cups**

  Metal measuring spoons are stronger than plastic and last longer. You should have two sets of measuring cups, one for dry ingredients and one for liquids (these have a spout).

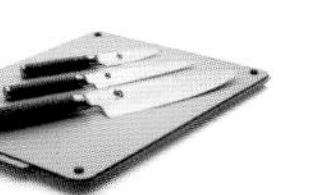

- **Flexible Cutting Board**

  Many cooks swear by their wooden boards, but I like the ability to move quickly in the kitchen. You can pick up a flexible board and scrape the cut ingredients directly into the pot. Look for a color-coordinated set of cutting boards to reduce the risk of cross-contamination.

Melamine Mixing Bowls

Glass and ceramic mixing bowls are fine, but I love my melamine bowls. I've had them for a decade. Look for bowls that have a rubber bottom edge to reduce the slip factor. They should be deep enough for splatter control and wide enough to allow for whisking.

Baking Sheet

Not just for cookies: it's easy to lay out recipe ingredients, roast vegetables, and do more on a baking sheet. A 1-inch rimmed half-sheet pan (18 x 13 inches) works well (as long as it fits into your oven). I often line mine with parchment paper for easy cleanup.

Mesh Strainer

I call this my Sunday tool: once I'm home from the market, I put it in the sink for when I scrub vegetables and wash fruit. A medium strainer, large enough to hold 2 pounds of strawberries, works well for many tasks.

Tongs

If you want to up-level your kitchen "cred," buy a pair of tongs. They make you seem like you really know what you are doing in the kitchen, and they can flip burgers, toss salads, turn shrimp, scrape browned bits out of a pot, and work as a serving tool at dinnertime. I use rubber-tipped tongs so my lovely pans do not scratch. Make sure they have a spring action for quick one-handed open and close.

Silicone Spoon Spatula

This tool is as useful for sautéing vegetables as it is for stirring morning oatmeal. Mine have wooden handles and come in bright colors, reminding me to have fun in the kitchen.

Flat Wooden Spatula

The ultimate multitasker, this utensil is a tried-and-true friend in the kitchen. Round spoons can't get into the corners of a saucepan and metal spatulas are rough on cookware. My wooden spatulas are well worn. I wouldn't even consider making soup, stew, or sautéed onions without one.

Vegetable Peeler

My five-year-old is the official peeler in our household. He's tenacious about little spots and imperfections, which are quickly removed with a swipe of his peeler. Look for one with a good grip and a blade opening at least 3 inches wide. Oxo and KitchenAid both make excellent, durable peelers.

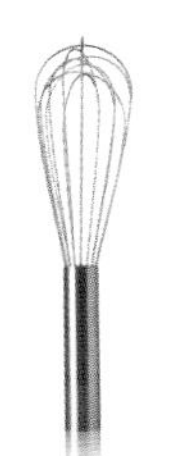

Whisk

For me, a balloon whisk takes up too much space in the utensil drawer; I prefer the versatile longer, thinner French whisk. I use it for beating eggs, making dressings, and whipping cream. No matter which type you prefer, don't skimp on quality. A strong stainless-steel whisk with a solid round handle will make for easy work.

Kitchen Shears

I cut everything with kitchen shears: herbs, lettuce, pasta, chicken, even meat. Once you start using kitchen shears, you will find thousands of tasks for them. Keep a dedicated kitchen pair away from art projects, which will dull the shears.

Grater

A stainless-steel grater does more than grate Parmesan. Microplane is my go-to brand for quality and durability. It can grate onions, carrots, and chocolate too. I get the most use out of a grater with a 3-inch-wide blade and a long, removable handle. You can also use a box grater.

KNIVES

Selecting knives can be overwhelming. The three most important factors to consider:

Blade: For sturdiness, I prefer knives with the blade running the entire length of the knife, through the handle.

Handle: A good grip is crucial, so consider the size and weight of the handle. Don't let the handle weigh down your hand: it should have a nice balance with the blade.

Weight: If a knife is too heavy, each cut is a burden; too light, and you both lose control over the blade and must put more force into cutting.

Knife fanatics will defend their favorite brand, but I use several brands to round out my collection. Shun is a favorite, but Wüsthof is a more economical option for home cooks. Choose the knife that suits you, and don't skimp on quality; even if you can purchase just one, make it count.

- **8-Inch Chef's Knife**
  There is no single tool for cooking that you will rely on more than a sharp chef's knife.

- **6-Inch Serrated Knife**
  A serrated knife blade cuts through tomatoes like a charm and does double duty on bread and tough-skinned vegetables like squash.

- **4-Inch Paring Knife**
  The pointed tip of a slender paring knife gets into tight spaces a larger chef's knife cannot touch. It's perfect for slicing smaller fruits and vegetables, such as strawberries and garlic.

POTS AND PANS

Unless you happen to have a sous chef as your best friend, you will rely on pots and pans to do most of the work in your kitchen. A good pan can last decades if treated with care and washed quickly after cooking. Because pots and pans can be a sizable investment, I prefer to purchase them "à la carte," rather than a set, which often come with a few you will never touch. Keep your eye out for sales at home goods discount stores or online via eBay or brand websites looking to liquidate last year's models.

• 10- to 12-Inch Skillet

The all-purpose pan. Skillets have slanted edges and are always measured in inches across the top, while sauté pan edges are straight and size is described as a volume measure. Most of The Fresh 20 recipes that use a skillet call for a 10- to 12-inch (medium) pan. Invest in quality. For more recommendations, visit www.thefresh20.com.

• 8-Quart Stockpot

There are a lot of things you can prepare with a sturdy stockpot. My kids think it is for popcorn, but my soups, pastas, and corn on the cob know different. I like a heavy-bottomed 18/10 grade stainless-steel pot. Some come with useful steamer inserts. If you have an old copper pot from your grandma, consider yourself lucky: they don't make them like they did in the old days.

• 2-Quart Saucepan

Use this versatile little pan to reheat rice, warm broth, and even melt butter for popcorn! My preference is an ovenproof, nonstick stainless-steel pot with a long handle and a tight-fitting lid.

• Dutch Oven

There are few things more beautiful than an afternoon braise made in a good-quality Dutch oven. Heavy cast-iron pots with an enamel coating have excellent heat conduction, which can turn a simple cut of meat into an award-winning braise. Start with a 5-quart pot, which is small enough to make dinner for four but big enough to squeeze in a whole chicken.

WEDGEWOOD

my food JOURNEY

I'm a Midwest girl, born right in the middle of the nation's meat-and-potato belt, Minnesota.

Our weeknight dinner was panfried steak and spuds, hamburgers, "broasted" chicken, or overcooked pasta with Ragù tomato sauce. The dinner salad was iceberg lettuce, pale tomatoes, sliced cucumber, and dressing from a bottle or a packet of dry Italian seasonings. I was fascinated by the free cruet that came with packages of Good Seasonings dressing mix. My parents would let me add the oil and shake until blended. Our "fresh" dressing was always just inside the refrigerator door.

my mom

My family didn't fit into the traditional Midwestern cooking mold. I was a latch-key kid with two ambitious working parents, while most of my friends had stay-at-home moms who spent their days tending to the domestic needs of meals and carpool. My mother worked for Litton, a leader in the microwave oven industry, and the idea that vegetables could come from the freezer and be ready in three minutes suited her just fine.

Thankfully, my parents shared kitchen duty when I was young, and my father was a different sort of cook.

dancing with dad

His family came from Barbados and Louisiana. He grew up in a home where frozen food was unknown and shopping was done when there was money for food, day by day and with a fierce eye to quality and value. The middle child and the only boy in a family of four sisters, my father learned quickly about cooking and, perhaps out of fear of his sisters' response, he learned early on to be choosy about ingredients. Surrounded by women talking and cooking and taking great pride in making something big and wonderful from a little bit of food, he developed an instinct for bringing the flavor out of any ingredient. It was not uncommon to see my dad spending an entire day preparing a meal.

It didn't matter that my family shared two styles of cooking. Either way, I loved to eat. My mother cooked out of necessity. She entertained for the company, not the food. My dad cooked to please himself and took more care in the preparation. Today I do both.

My passion for cooking comes from the paternal side of my family. I absorbed the excitement my father and his sisters had for cooking well and eating with relish. Late at night, when my father was seized by a craving for spicy homemade sausage, I rode shotgun to the hot-links outpost he frequented. On weekends, I loved it when my family visited his eldest sister, Anita.

Auntie Neats was married to a professional football player, and on many weekends, she

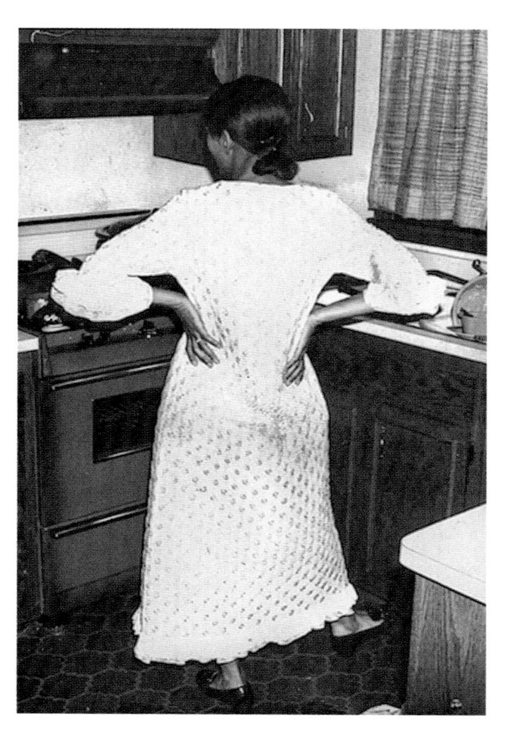

neats after the party

entertained the other players' families—fifty to a hundred people. Her kitchen was like nothing I'd ever seen in Minneapolis. Ham hocks, collard greens, chicken feet, okra, and chitterlings were on the stove in giant well-worn pots.

She poured champagne into Baccarat flutes, stirring the gumbo at the same time.

Her first words upon arrival were always "You hungry?"

Auntie Neats's kitchen was another world and I was enchanted. My sister immediately dashed upstairs to join our cousins playing away from the kitchen. I climbed up on a barstool and hovered, curiously, over the stove.

"You want to stir that pot for me, Missy?" she'd ask.

I was the only child among all the guests who was fascinated by Auntie Neats's kitchen magic, so I got special attention. It was an extension course in food education.

In 1982, my family moved to Southern California, where it was easier to eat fresh food—arugula, radicchio, basil and cilantro, ginger, salsa and guacamole, and other things unknown to me in Minneapolis were in every grocery store. In the 1980s, people were talking about food, celebrating it. My mother caught the bug, and by the time I was in high school, she and I became avid foodies, seeking out the best sushi, the best Thai noodles, and the finest French and Italian restaurants, leaving the microwave behind.

Sharing the pursuit of fine food forged an amazing bond. I can't imagine that I will ever be closer to another person in my life. We were best friends, and I often think of her when I cook.

For much of my life, eating was comfort. And by the time my teenage years arrived, I was a stark contrast to my size-4 mother and sister. I developed a secret junk food habit. When I was alone, I overindulged. The heavier I got, the more I tried to soothe myself with food. My "best friends" were Kraft macaroni and cheese, SpaghettiOs, Frosted Flakes, and Betty Crocker boxed brownies.

When I went to Paris for my junior year abroad, I had made peace with wearing plus sizes.

But I returned a year later a thinner version of myself. Living in a culture where quality of food trumped quantity changed everything.

But the junk food crept back in once I returned to California, especially when I was working as an interactive director in the corporate world, where I devoted myself to my job, leaving little time to put thought or care into what I ate. The easiest way to feed myself on hectic days filled with meetings and deadlines? Microwave-ready burritos. For many years my weight fluctuated, but then two distinct life experiences changed my food culture. I married and started having children. And my mother was diagnosed with a terminal illness and, for the last five years of her life, took all her nourishment through a feeding tube.

At first, the scent of freshly baked bread would tempt her to break her doctor's orders, but in time she made peace with the cruel hand she had been dealt. I watched as she severed her relationship with food, and I started having trouble being unconscious about what I was putting in my own body. I could not see my mother deprived of the joy of eating and squander my own ability to choose well and celebrate every bite. I could not see the babies in my arms and imagine feeding them anything but the best food. I could not imagine building a family that didn't eat together every night and share the bond that comes from that ritual.

It was that simple. I understood in a flash that life is composed of only so many meals, and I wanted as many of them as possible to sustain my body, my soul, and the life of my own family, as well as my family of friends. I believe my mom, who passed away in 2005, would approve.

It's not easy to achieve this. Everybody works too much; we all have too little time and, often, too little money. Rushing through the grocery store and throwing together meals had me serving stress instead of order and a nurturing serenity to my family. So in 2006, I began planning my weekly meals, and over several years, I found the combination of planning and whimsy that makes my life easier, more affordable, and more enjoyable—and lots healthier. That discovery is The Fresh 20.

IN SEASON

- Artichokes
- Arugula (wild)
- Asparagus
- Avocados
- Cucumbers
- Kale
- Kiwis
- Leeks
- Napa cabbage
- Navel oranges
- New potatoes
- Radishes
- Snow peas
- Baby spinach
- Sugar snap peas
- Swiss chard

SPRING

I fell in love with my husband in the spring, and three years later we were married in the lush garden behind my sister's house in the Los Angeles hills. Spring is special to me. When we were growing up in snowy Minnesota, the return of green grass was like waking from a long white haze. The shedding of winter coats meant that the thaw had arrived. Bye-bye snow boots and baked squash.

But even in a mild climate without melting snow, spring announces itself. The air smells of fresh lilacs and freesia, and beginning the last week of March, the roses in my front yard remind me that the first local asparagus, rhubarb, and globe artichokes are on their way.

There is something liberating about the season. People move from inside their houses to the patio, thoughts shift away from introspection.

In The Fresh 20 kitchen, spring is less about the dry heat of the oven and more about moist-heat cooking methods. Steaming is spring's savior. I trade in my heavy-duty Dutch oven for my sturdy 12-inch sauté pan and the promise of perfectly browned vegetables.

Fish has a big place on our spring table. In this chapter, I share recipes for balsamic-poached salmon, orange jalapeño shrimp, and coconut curry-style fish fillets. In April, we always look forward to a lamb dinner—I love using ground lamb at this time of year because it is easier to cook with during the week than a whole roast. We turn away from winter roasts and look to the skillet, where we find Korean-style short ribs, sautéed chicken, quick-baked Parmesan chicken nuggets, and grilled pork chops.

For me, spring is a soft suggestion to lighten up and reactivate.

If summer is family time, autumn is back to school, and winter is introspection, spring is community and reconnection. The farmers' markets reopen. The light is back, days begin to lengthen, and hearts thaw.

SPRING MENU

WEEK 1

MONDAY

Parmesan Chicken Nuggets
with Herbed Honey-Glazed Carrots

TUESDAY

Coconut Curry-Style Fish
with Lime Coconut Rice

WEDNESDAY

Korean-Style Short Ribs
with Braised Napa Cabbage
and Brown Rice

THURSDAY

Pan-Seared Chicken Panzanella

FRIDAY

Baked Potato Soup
with Simple Salad

SHOPPING LIST

Meat/Seafood

4 boneless, skinless chicken breasts (about 2½ pounds)

1¼ pounds boneless, skinless fish fillets (any variety), at least 1 inch thick

2 pounds beef short ribs, cross-cut into 1-inch-thick slabs, Korean-style (ask the butcher to cut the ribs)

Optional: 8 ounces uncured bacon (see Baked Potato Soup, page 15)

**Note: Choose an all-natural nitrate-free uncured bacon like Niman Ranch.*

Vegetables/Fruit

One 2-inch piece fresh ginger

8 medium carrots

2 medium red onions

1 bunch fresh chives

2 pounds Dutch Baby or new potatoes

2 pints grape or cherry tomatoes

3 medium celery stalks

1 head Napa cabbage

4 ounces baby arugula (about 8 cups lightly packed)

3 limes, juiced

3 navel oranges

Dairy

¾ cup grated Parmesan cheese (about 3 ounces)

1 large egg

Optional: 1 cup shredded raw-milk cheddar cheese

Bakery/Misc.

1 whole wheat baguette

2 Tablespoons sesame oil

2½ cups coconut milk

From the Pantry

5 Tablespoons plus ⅓ cup olive oil

3 Tablespoons grapeseed oil

2 Tablespoons white wine vinegar

¼ cup balsamic vinegar

¼ cup reduced-sodium soy sauce

4 cups low-sodium chicken or vegetable broth

3¼ teaspoons kosher salt

2¼ teaspoons black pepper

5 teaspoons dried oregano

¾ teaspoon cayenne pepper

½ teaspoon herbes de Provence

1 teaspoon ground cumin

7 garlic cloves

3 Tablespoons honey

2 Tablespoons whole wheat flour

2 cups brown rice (dry)

1 teaspoon Dijon mustard

PREP AHEAD

Brown Rice for Tuesday and Wednesday

Prepare 4 cups brown rice (see page xvii).

Marinated Short Ribs for Wednesday

¼ cup reduced-sodium soy sauce

2 Tablespoons honey

2 Tablespoons sesame oil

½ medium red onion, finely chopped

3 garlic cloves, minced or pressed

1 Tablespoon olive oil

2 Tablespoons white wine vinegar

2 pounds beef short ribs, cross-cut into 1-inch-thick slabs, Korean-style

1. Combine marinade ingredients in a non-aluminum container. Cover and refrigerate.

2. The morning of the dinner, add ribs to marinade and turn to coat well. Seal container and place in fridge for at least 2 hours and up to 24 hours.

Bread Crumbs for Monday
Bread Cubes for Thursday

1 whole wheat baguette (half cut into long, thin strips, half cut into large 2-inch cubes)

1 Tablespoon olive oil

1 teaspoon dried oregano

¼ teaspoon kosher salt

¼ teaspoon black pepper

1. Preheat the broiler and place a rack 6 inches from the heat.

2. Toss the bread cubes with the oil, oregano, salt, and pepper. Arrange the seasoned cubes on one half of the baking sheet in an even layer. Place the unseasoned strips on the other half.

3. Toast under the broiler for 3 to 5 minutes, until golden.

4. Turn the cubes once or twice to avoid burning.

5. Place the cubes in a sealed container for use later in the week.

6. Grind the strips in a food processor or blender until mealy.

7. Transfer to a sealed container or baggie for use later in the week.

Dressing for Thursday and Friday

3 Tablespoons balsamic vinegar
2 garlic cloves, minced or pressed
1 teaspoon dried oregano
1 teaspoon Dijon mustard
½ teaspoon kosher salt
½ teaspoon black pepper
9 Tablespoons olive oil

Whisk together all the ingredients in a bowl until combined. Store the dressing in an airtight container in the refrigerator for up to 7 days. Shake well before serving.

Yield: ¾ cup

fish selection

Finding good-quality seafood can be a challenge in some areas. And so much of our fish supply is brought in from overseas, where regulations are not as strict and the amount of pollutants is likely higher. When possible, purchase fresh open-water fish from a reputable fishmonger. According to the Monterey Bay Aquarium, which keeps a watch on sustainable fish, some of the healthiest choices are Alaskan salmon, yellowfin tuna, U.S.-farmed tilapia, and Pacific halibut. If your only option is farmed fish, always make sure it is from the United States. Check out the aquarium's Seafood Watch for more information.

Find a good-quality source for fish, even if it is mail-order, and stick with it. When buying fish, don't be afraid to ask questions about texture, flavor, and overall "fishiness." If you are unfamiliar with fish, start with a mild species such as cod or tilapia, and work up to freshly caught lake trout or catfish, which can have a stronger flavor. Look for firm flesh that is not at all slimy. A thicker fish with a dense consistency will hold up well when cooking and not fall apart.

Spring Week 1: Monday

PARMESAN CHICKEN NUGGETS

with Herbed Honey-Glazed Carrots

If you have kids, chances are your household is familiar with chicken nuggets. For quality control, skip the frozen meat version and prepare them at home instead. I've fed dozens of kids this recipe and received the highest praise from a five-year-old, who told me they tasted better than the Golden Arches version. For best results, use fine-quality Parmigiano-Reggiano as your Parmesan.

Serves 4: 30 minutes

for the honey-glazed carrots

6 medium carrots, peeled and cut into ¼-inch slices

1 Tablespoon olive oil

1 Tablespoon honey

½ teaspoon herbes de Provence

½ teaspoon kosher salt

¼ teaspoon black pepper

for the parmesan chicken nuggets

1 Tablespoon olive oil

2 boneless, skinless chicken breasts (about 1¼ pounds)

½ teaspoon kosher salt

¼ teaspoon black pepper

1 large egg

¼ cup water

1 cup Bread Crumbs (see Prep Ahead, page 4)

½ cup grated Parmesan

1 teaspoon dried oregano

¼ teaspoon cayenne pepper

on the side

2 navel oranges, cut into wedges

Preheat the oven to 375°F.

for the honey-glazed carrots

1. In a small bowl, combine the carrots with the olive oil, honey, herbes, salt, and pepper, tossing to coat. Arrange the carrots on one side of the baking sheet, leaving room for the chicken nuggets. Set aside.

for the parmesan chicken nuggets

1. Lightly coat a baking sheet with the olive oil.
2. Cut the chicken into small cubes; each breast should yield 12 pieces, and the cubes should be similar in size for even cooking. Sprinkle the chicken with the salt and pepper.
3. In a small bowl, whisk together the egg and water.
4. In a medium dish, combine the bread crumbs, Parmesan, oregano, and cayenne pepper.
5. Using a fork or chopsticks, one piece at a time, dip the chicken into the egg mix and then roll in the crumb mix, making sure it is evenly coated. Lay the chicken on the baking sheet, leaving space between the pieces.
6. Place the chicken in the oven, along with the carrots (above), and cook for about 15 minutes, until the chicken is no longer pink on the inside and the carrots are tender. Turn nuggets halfway through.
7. Serve with a side of orange wedges.

COCONUT CURRY-STYLE FISH

with Lime Coconut Rice

Sometimes parents have to "convince" kids to eat fish for dinner. Let me introduce you to an easy sell: the sweet, fragrant coconut neutralizes the strong smell of the fish. Expect repeat requests for this dish.

Serves 4: 35 minutes  

for the coconut curry-style fish

- 1¼ pounds boneless, skinless fish fillets (any variety), at least 1 inch thick
- 1 Tablespoon grapeseed oil
- ½ medium red onion, finely chopped
- 1 teaspoon grated fresh ginger
- 2 garlic cloves, minced or pressed
- 1 pint grape or cherry tomatoes, cut in half
- 1 teaspoon ground cumin
- ½ teaspoon kosher salt
- ¼ teaspoon black pepper
- ½ teaspoon cayenne pepper
- 1½ cups coconut milk
- 1 Tablespoon finely chopped fresh chives

for the lime coconut rice

- 1 cup coconut milk
- 2 limes, juiced
- ¼ teaspoon kosher salt
- 2 cups prepared brown rice

for the coconut curry-style fish

1. Wash the fish and pat very dry. Cut into 2-inch pieces.
2. Heat the oil in a medium saucepan over medium-high heat. Add the onion, ginger, and garlic and sauté until softened, about 3 minutes.
3. Add the tomatoes and sauté for another 3 minutes, stirring frequently to break up the tomatoes.
4. Add the cumin, salt, black pepper, and cayenne. Stir to combine, and cook for 2 minutes.
5. Add the coconut milk. Bring to a simmer, add the fish, and cook for 3 to 5 minutes, depending on the thickness of the fish, until the fish is opaque throughout.
6. Serve over rice with a sprinkle of chives as garnish.

for the lime coconut rice

1. Bring the coconut milk, lime juice, and salt to a low simmer.
2. Stir in the prepared brown rice and cook for 5 minutes until heated through and some of the liquid is absorbed.

Spring Week I: Tuesday

Spring Week I: Wednesday

KOREAN-STYLE SHORT RIBS

with Braised Napa Cabbage and Brown Rice

The cut on these ribs makes for quick cooking. Ask your butcher for "flanken-style" ribs cut about 1 inch thick and three rib bones across. For tender results, I like to marinate overnight. This subscriber favorite is a good recipe to double. I hope your family can keep it friendly when there is only one rib left.

Serves 4: 30 minutes  

Marinated Short Ribs (see Prep Ahead, p. 4)

1 cup low-sodium chicken or vegetable broth

½ head Napa cabbage, shredded

2 medium carrots, grated or shredded

2 cups prepared brown rice

1. Remove the ribs from the marinade, reserving the marinade, and arrange in a large sauté pan (with a lid). Set over medium-high heat and sear for about 4 minutes each side, until the ribs are browned.

2. Pour the reserved marinade and the broth into the pan, cover, reduce the heat to medium-low, and cook for 15 minutes.

3. Remove the lid and cook, uncovered, for 5 minutes to reduce the liquid. Transfer the ribs to a platter or serving dish and cover loosely with foil. Save the rest of the cooking liquid to serve alongside the ribs.

4. Add the cabbage and carrots to the pan, stirring to combine, and cook over medium heat until wilted. Add to the serving platter.

5. Heat brown rice over medium heat with 2 Tablespoons water. Fluff with fork and serve on the side.

PAN-SEARED CHICKEN PANZANELLA

Traditionally, panzanella is made using stale bread. I prefer to toast fresh bread. Citrus adds just the right amount of sweetness to balance the salt of the chicken and the bread. Arugula can be strong for young palates. A lettuce blend works well as an alternative.

Serves 4: 25 minutes

2 boneless, skinless chicken breasts (about 1¼ pounds), cut lengthwise in half

½ teaspoon kosher salt

½ teaspoon black pepper

1 Tablespoon olive oil

Bread Cubes (see Prep Ahead, page 4)

4 ounces baby arugula (about 8 cups lightly packed)

1 navel orange, peeled and sliced

1 pint grape or cherry tomatoes, cut in half

¼ cup grated Parmesan cheese

¼ cup Dressing (see Prep Ahead, p. 5)

1. Pat the chicken dry with paper towels and season with the salt and pepper. Heat the oil in a 12-inch skillet over medium-high heat. Add the chicken and brown on both sides, about 5 minutes each. Transfer the chicken to a cutting board and let cool slightly.

2. Cut the chicken into 1-inch cubes.

3. In a medium salad bowl, combine the toasted bread cubes, chicken, arugula, orange, tomatoes, and cheese. Toss with the desired amount of dressing.

Spring Week I:
Thursday

BAKED POTATO SOUP

with Simple Salad

I wanted to lighten up the traditional cream-laden potato soup for spring. All the important flavors are here, but I feel energetic instead of heavy after eating a large bowl. On weeknights when schedules are complicated, a pot of soup is the perfect solution to varying dinner times. Hide any leftovers for yourself; this soup tastes even better the second day.

Serves 4: 35 minutes

- 2 Tablespoons grapeseed oil
- 1 medium red onion, finely chopped
- 3 medium celery stalks, finely chopped
- 2 Tablespoons whole wheat flour
- 2 teaspoons dried oregano
- ½ teaspoon kosher salt
- 2 pounds Baby Dutch or new potatoes, peeled and cut into ½-inch cubes
- 3 cups low-sodium chicken or vegetable broth
- 1 cup water
- 1 Tablespoon fresh lime juice
- ¼ teaspoon black pepper
- ¼ cup finely chopped fresh chives
- 8 ounces uncured bacon, cooked and crumbled until crisp (optional)
- 1 cup shredded raw-milk cheddar cheese (optional)
- ½ head Napa cabbage, shredded
- ½ cup dressing (see Prep Ahead, page 5)

1. Heat the oil in a medium pot over medium-high heat. Add the onion and celery and sauté until softened, about 5 minutes.

2. Stir in the flour and cook until the raw flour smell has gone away, about 2 minutes. Season with the oregano and salt, then add the potatoes and cook for 3 minutes.

3. Add the broth, water, and lime juice and stir until well blended. Bring to a simmer for 15 minutes, or until the potatoes are fork-tender and the soup has thickened.

4. Divide the soup into 4 bowls and garnish with a sprinkle of black pepper and chives.

Optional: If adding bacon, sprinkle on top. If adding cheese, stir in to combine and melt.

5. Toss cabbage and dressing for a simple side salad.

sub rice flour for flour and use gluten-free broth

omit cheese

omit bacon and cheese and use vegetable broth

FAMILY FOOD CULTURE
Moderation
the lanz family

TRENT, photographer/industrial designer MELISSA, founder of The Fresh 20

AIDEN AND ELIOTT, the sunshine boys

I want my family to be healthy, vibrant, and strong. My little ones enjoy wholesome food and know there is a deep connection between what they eat and how they feel. Yes, sometimes there is a plea for treats, but my family food culture centers on moderation. We eat fresh because it feels good, and there is never a sense that we are giving up something by skipping processed foods. Together we have set up food habits that are sustainable and require nothing more than planning ahead and the desire to live healthy.

Trent has always been food conscious. He suffers from a salt affinity and on rare occasions arrives home with a bag of sunflower seeds, but day to day, he makes solid choices about food. Heart disease runs in Trent's family, so a healthy diet low in sodium is all the more important. His favorite vegetable is corn, and the pasta bowl should never be left directly in front of him if we want leftovers.

In the not too distant past, my own idea of a complete meal was a frozen bean and cheese burrito with a packet of hot sauce. I also have a weakness for French cheeses. For me, every day is a chance to cultivate happiness in my kitchen, and healthy food plays a big role. Plus, I eat well because my kids are watching. My favorite vegetable is guacamole.

At eight, Aiden is a self-proclaimed hot-dog-atarian. He leans toward a healthy portion of vegetables at dinner and generally steers clear of fatty meats. Birthday-party hot dogs are his weakness and he is allowed to indulge every once in a while. Raised on organic vegetables and lean proteins, Aiden has a solid understanding of the food cycle and prefers fish to meat. His favorite vegetable is tomato.

Eliott eats anything and everything. His appetite is healthy and he is willing to try new things. He is a superb little chef in the kitchen and enjoys getting his hands dirty with food prep. As he grows, so will the grocery bill, so teaching Eliott about portions and making healthy choices is a large part of our family food culture. His favorite vegetable is salad.

lanz family food culture

SPECIAL OR RESTRICTED DIET: None

WHO COOKS MOST MEALS?: Melissa and little man Eliott

FAVORITE FAMILY MEAL: Pasta

LEAST FAVORITE MEAL: Stir-fry

STRICT RULE: No soda!

INDULGENCE: Doughnut Sunday (once a month)

BEST ADVICE FOR HEALTH: Portion control

HARDEST TREAT TO GIVE UP: Ice cream

ON THE NO-EAT LIST: Okra

SPRING MENU

MONDAY

Greek-Style Lamb Tacos
with Cucumber Yogurt Sauce and Salad

TUESDAY

Orange Jalapeño Shrimp
with Broccoli and Brown Rice

WEDNESDAY

Chicken Satay
with Peanut Noodles and Cucumber Salad

THURSDAY

Guacamole Tostadas
with Fried Eggs

FRIDAY

Lamb Penne
with Simple Green Salad

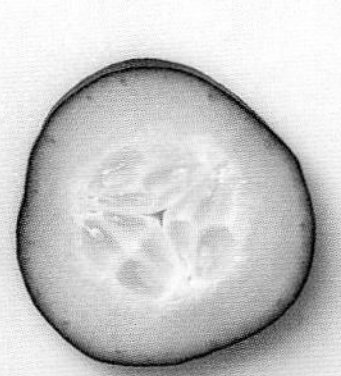

SHOPPING LIST

Meat/Seafood

2 pounds ground lamb

2 boneless, skinless chicken breasts (about 1¼ pounds)

1 pound raw deveined shrimp, tail on

Vegetables/Fruit

1 medium red onion

3 red bell peppers

1 bunch fresh flat-leaf parsley

2 heads butter lettuce, such as Bibb

3 small limes

2 avocados

2 medium cucumbers

One 3-inch piece of fresh ginger

1 small jalapeño pepper

8 ounces broccoli florets (about 3 cups)

5 navel oranges

Dairy

4 large eggs

1 cup shredded raw-milk cheddar cheese

1 cup plain nonfat Greek yogurt

Bakery/Misc.

12 corn tortillas, 6-inch size (see DIY Corn Tortillas, pages 105–6)

Two 15-ounce cans kidney beans

¼ cup creamy peanut butter

From the Pantry

3 Tablespoons plus ½ cup grapeseed oil

3 Tablespoons olive oil

3⅝ teaspoons kosher salt

1¼ teaspoons black pepper

¼ teaspoon cayenne pepper

1½ teaspoons ground cumin

1 teaspoon dried oregano

1 teaspoon white wine vinegar

1 cup low-sodium chicken or vegetable broth

8 garlic cloves

5 Tablespoons honey

7 Tablespoons plus 2 teaspoons reduced-sodium soy sauce

8 ounces whole wheat penne

8 ounces whole wheat spaghetti

1 cup brown rice (dry)

4 Tablespoons Pantry Dressing of your choice (pages 26–7)

PREP AHEAD

Cucumber Yogurt Sauce for Monday

1 medium cucumber, peeled

1 cup plain nonfat Greek yogurt

Juice of 1 lime

½ bunch fresh flat-leaf parsley

¼ teaspoon kosher salt

1. Shred half of the cucumber.
2. Cut the other half into a small ½-inch dice.
3. Combine the shredded cucumber, yogurt, and lime juice.
4. Mix in the diced cucumber and parsley.
5. Add in the kosher salt.
6. Chill until ready to serve (up to 3 days).

Yield: 2 cups

Brown Rice for Tuesday

Prepare 2 cups brown rice (see page xvii).

Marinated Chicken for Wednesday

⅓ cup reduced-sodium soy sauce

½ cup grapeseed oil

2 Tablespoons grated fresh ginger

2 garlic cloves, minced or pressed

1 teaspoon ground cumin

¼ teaspoon black pepper

2 boneless, skinless chicken breasts (about 1¼ pounds), cut into 3-inch strips

Note: Prepare the marinade up to 3 days in advance but only add chicken the night before or the morning of dinner.

1. Combine all the ingredients, except the chicken, together in a large non-aluminum container. Refrigerate up to 3 days.
2. The night before or the morning of dinner, add the chicken to the marinade and coat well. Seal the container and marinate in the refrigerator for at least 1 hour and up to 24 hours.

a fresh idea:

GLOBAL TACOS

Taco night is a lifesaver for busy families. Every culture has its own variation on tacos. Middle Eastern pitas or lavash, Indian naan, and Mexican tortillas can be stuffed with any leftover meat, vegetables, or legumes. Add a sauce, and you are on your way to an easy handheld meal.

Spring Week II: Monday

GREEK-STYLE LAMB TACOS

with Cucumber Yogurt Sauce and Salad

I introduced my kids to this ground lamb before moving on to the more distinctive flavor of lamb chops and roasts. They call it the "good ground beef" and ask for these tacos often during the spring. I implore you to try it before assuming the kids won't enjoy this tender meat. Many are happily surprised.

Serves 4: 20 minutes 

for the lamb tacos

1 Tablespoon grapeseed oil

½ medium red onion, finely chopped

1 pound ground lamb

1 teaspoon kosher salt

½ teaspoon black pepper

½ teaspoon ground cumin

1 teaspoon dried oregano

8 corn tortillas, 6-inch taco size

2 cups Cucumber Yogurt Sauce (see Prep Ahead, page 20)

1 red bell pepper, cored, seeded, and chopped

for the salad

½ head butter lettuce, such as Bibb, washed and chopped

1 navel orange, peeled and chopped

2 Tablespoons Pantry Dressing of your choice (pages 26–7)

Dash of black pepper

for the lamb tacos

1. Heat a 10- to 12-inch skillet over medium heat and add the oil. Add the onion and sauté until softened, 3 to 4 minutes.
2. Add the ground lamb and season with the salt, pepper, cumin, and oregano, stirring to combine. Cook until the lamb is browned and no longer pink inside, 3 to 4 minutes. Remove from the heat. If necessary, drain a little fat from the pan or blot it up with a paper towel.
3. To soften, heat the tortillas wrapped in wet paper towels in the microwave for 30 seconds, or place one by one in a lightly oiled pan and heat for 10 seconds per side.
4. Spoon 3 Tablespoons of the lamb into each tortilla followed by 2 Tablespoons of the yogurt sauce. Top with the chopped bell pepper.
5. Arrange the tacos on a serving platter.

for the salad

In a large salad bowl, combine the lettuce, chopped oranges, and dressing. Sprinkle with the black pepper.

 omit yogurt sauce and serve with cucumber sticks

ORANGE JALAPEÑO SHRIMP

with Broccoli and Brown Rice

Serving shrimp for dinner means you can have a meal on the table in ten minutes. This recipe uses navel oranges for a sweet, tangy glaze. If you prefer, substitute cubed organic chicken tenders, which will cook just as quickly. Serve ingredients in separate bowls and have everyone create their own rice bowl.

Serves 4: 25 minutes  

- 1 pound raw deveined shrimp, tails on
- ¾ teaspoon kosher salt
- ¼ teaspoon black pepper
- Juice of 3 navel oranges (¾ cup)
- 2 Tablespoons honey
- 1 teaspoon reduced-sodium soy sauce
- 1 Tablespoon grapeseed oil
- 1 small jalapeño pepper, seeded and finely chopped (about 2 teaspoons)
- 2 garlic cloves, minced
- 8 ounces broccoli florets (about 3 cups)
- 1 navel orange, peeled and sectioned
- 2 cups prepared brown rice, reheated (see Prep Ahead)

1. Season the shrimp with salt and pepper. Set aside.

2. Bring the orange juice, honey, and soy sauce to a boil in a small saucepan over high heat and boil until reduced by about half, about 8 minutes. Set aside.

3. Heat a large skillet over medium heat and add the grapeseed oil. Add the jalapeño and garlic and cook for 2 minutes.

4. Toss in the shrimp and cook until the shrimp start to turn opaque, using tongs to toss the shrimp so they cook evenly.

5. Add the orange juice reduction and cook for 3 to 4 minutes. Lift the shrimp out of the pan, leaving the liquid behind.

6. Add the broccoli florets and orange sections to the pan and cook for about 4 minutes, until the broccoli is just tender.

7. Add the shrimp back into the pan, stirring to combine, and serve over the brown rice.

 Substitute tofu for the shrimp. Cut the tofu into 2-inch cubes.

Spring Week II: Tuesday

Homemade salad dressings can transform a plain salad into a masterpiece with a prep time of less than five minutes. It takes longer to choose one in the grocery aisle! Flexible and fresh, they are an essential ingredient in an unprocessed kitchen. What follows are my most-used dressings, the basis for most of my other dressings. Use an olive oil that is not too heavy; invest in a good oil for dressings, but don't break the bank cooking with an oil that is meant for a delicate finishing drizzle.

In general, the ratio for dressings is 3 parts oil, 1 part vinegar.

Basic Vinaigrette

Let the kids help—there is very little room for error if you add ingredients a little at a time and to taste.

- 1 Tablespoon balsamic vinegar
- ½ teaspoon Dijon mustard
- ¼ teaspoon kosher salt
- ⅛ teaspoon black pepper
- 3 Tablespoons olive oil

Whisk all the ingredients together in a small bowl until smooth. Store the vinaigrette in an airtight container in the refrigerator for up to 2 weeks.

Honey Mustard Dressing

- ¼ cup mayonnaise
- ¼ cup olive oil
- 2 teaspoons Dijon mustard
- 2 Tablespoons honey

Whisk all the ingredients together in a small bowl until well blended. Store the dressing in an airtight container in the refrigerator for up to 3 days.

Italian Dressing

¼ cup olive oil

1 garlic clove, minced or pressed

1 teaspoon dried oregano, crumbled between your fingers

2 Tablespoons balsamic vinegar

1 Tablespoon honey

Whisk all the ingredients together in a small bowl until smooth. Store the dressing in an airtight container in the refrigerator for up to 2 weeks.

Mayonnaise

Mayonnaise is a little tricky, but homemade versions are far superior to what is available at the corner market. The egg yolks must be at room temperature to start!

2 large egg yolks, at room temperature

1 teaspoon Dijon mustard

1 teaspoon fresh lemon juice

⅓ cup grapeseed oil

½ cup olive oil

½ teaspoon kosher salt

1. With a handheld mixer, beat the yolks, mustard, and lemon juice in a small bowl until well blended and light in color, about 1 minute.

2. Very slowly drizzle in the oil, a small amount at a time, beating until the mayo thickens and emulsifies. If done right, it may take you up to 3 minutes to add all the oil. Patience wins! Then beat until stiff peaks form.

3. Add the salt and mix well. Store the mayonnaise in an airtight container in the refrigerator for up to 3 days.

Spring Week II: Wednesday

CHICKEN SATAY

with Peanut Noodles and Cucumber Salad

Food on a stick is always popular with kids. The fragrant ginger in the marinade gives the chicken a fresh spring vibe. Those with peanut allergies can skip the sauce. Dip in mustard instead. Don't worry about the skewers if you do not have any on hand—the chicken can be grilled flat in a pinch. See grilling indoors on page 66.

Serves 4: 25 minutes 

for the chicken satay

Marinated Chicken (see Prep Ahead, page 20)

Wooden skewers, soaked in cold water for 10 minutes

for the peanut noodles

2 pinches kosher salt for pasta water

8 ounces whole wheat spaghetti

½ lime, juiced

2 garlic cloves, minced or pressed

2 Tablespoons honey

¼ cup creamy peanut butter

⅔ cup hot water

2 Tablespoons reduced-sodium soy sauce

for the cucumber salad

1 medium cucumber, thinly sliced

1 teaspoon white wine vinegar

1 Tablespoon honey

Slight pinch of cayenne pepper

for the chicken satay

1. Preheat an outdoor grill to medium-high.
2. Skewer the marinated chicken on the soaked skewers; discard the marinade. Grill the chicken for about 3 to 4 minutes per side, until it's no longer pink in the middle.
3. Serve the chicken warm, with the peanut noodles.

for the peanut noodles

1. Fill a large pot with water, add 2 generous pinches of salt, and bring to a boil. Add the pasta and cook until al dente, 8 to 10 minutes.
2. Combine the lime juice, garlic, honey, peanut butter, hot water, and soy sauce in a small saucepan and bring to a simmer over low heat. Simmer for 3 to 5 minutes, stirring occasionally.
3. Drain the pasta and toss with half of the peanut sauce. Serve remaining sauce with satay.

for the cucumber salad

In a small bowl, toss the cucumber slices with the white wine vinegar, honey, and cayenne pepper.

 use 4 ounces rice noodles instead of spaghetti

 omit chicken satay

GUACAMOLE TOSTADAS

with Fried Eggs

I sometimes overlook eggs as a viable option for dinner, but they are easy to prepare in very little time. I would eat only guacamole for dinner if I could, but thanks to my inner health coach, I added kidney beans and eggs for balance. Once you have the hang of this recipe, it becomes an easy go-to meal for breakfast or lunch as well. You can use cilantro, spinach, and black beans as substitutes. It's flexible! Try it with homemade corn tortillas (page 105).

Serves 4: 30 minutes  

for the tortillas

4 corn tortillas, 6-inch size

2 Tablespoons olive oil

for the lettuce

½ head butter lettuce, such as Bibb, torn into small pieces

2 teaspoons fresh lime juice

¼ teaspoon kosher salt

1 Tablespoon finely chopped fresh flat-leaf parsley

for the guacamole

2 avocados, halved and pitted

¼ medium red onion, finely chopped

1 garlic clove, minced or pressed

½ teaspoon fresh lime juice

Kosher salt and black pepper

for the tortillas

1. Preheat the oven to 400°F.
2. Brush the tortillas with the olive oil on both sides. Arrange on a large baking sheet and bake, turning once, for 6 minutes, or until slightly browned. Set aside.

for the lettuce

In a small bowl, toss the lettuce with the lime juice, salt, and parsley. Set aside.

for the guacamole

Mash the avocados in a small bowl. Mix in the onion, garlic, and lime juice. Add salt and pepper to taste.

for the eggs

1 Tablespoon olive oil

4 large eggs

Two 15-ounce cans kidney beans, drained and rinsed

1 cup shredded raw-milk cheddar cheese

1 red bell pepper, cored, seeded, and finely chopped, optional

for the eggs

1. Heat the oil in a 10- to 12-inch skillet and fry the eggs to the desired doneness; I recommend over easy. Season the eggs.

2. To assemble the tostadas, layer the guacamole, kidney beans, and lettuce mixture on the tortillas, then top with the eggs, cheese, and optional red bell pepper. Yum. Just yum.

Spring Week II: Thursday

Spring Week II: Friday

LAMB PENNE

with Simple Green Salad

Friday evening is a wonderful time to pull together a quick pasta dish. But don't overload: to maintain good portion control, use 8 ounces of pasta for a family of four. If you make the whole pound, you will eat the whole pound. Substitute other fresh or dried herbs to customize the meal to your family's tastes—try thyme instead of parsley. And, if you prefer, use ground turkey instead of lamb.

Serves 4: 25 minutes 

for the lamb penne

1½ teaspoons kosher salt

8 ounces whole wheat penne

1 Tablespoon grapeseed oil

1 pound ground lamb

¼ medium red onion, chopped

1 garlic clove, minced

¼ teaspoon black pepper

1 red bell pepper, cored, seeded, and minced

½ cup chopped fresh flat-leaf parsley

1 cup low-sodium chicken or vegetable broth

for the simple green salad

1 head butter lettuce, such as Bibb, leaves separated, washed, dried, and torn into pieces

2 Tablespoons Pantry Dressing of your choice (pages 26–7)

Dash of black pepper

for the lamb penne

1. Fill a large pot with water, add 1 teaspoon of the salt, and bring to a boil. Add the pasta and cook until al dente, 8 to 12 minutes. Drain the pasta, reserving ½ cup of the pasta water. Return the pasta to the pot and keep warm.

Note: In general, I do not add oil to my pasta water. This lets the sauce stick more easily to the noodles.

2. Heat a large skillet over medium-high heat and add the oil. When the oil is hot, brown the lamb, about 5 minutes.

3. Add the onion, garlic, the remaining ½ teaspoon salt, and the pepper and cook for 2 to 3 minutes. Toss in the red pepper and parsley, then add the broth and the reserved pasta water and simmer gently over low heat for 4 to 5 minutes, until the pepper softens.

4. Add the lamb to the pasta and stir well. Divide among bowls and serve.

for the simple green salad

In a salad bowl, toss the lettuce with the dressing and sprinkle the pepper on top.

substitute gluten-free penne and gluten-free broth

SPRING MENU

Note: More and more, I am introducing vegetarian meals into my family food rotation. It's important to connect my kids with all kinds of produce. With these all-vegetarian recipes, protein-rich quinoa, hearty beans, and the king of veggies, the artichoke, come together for one satisfying week.

MONDAY

Red Beans and Quinoa

TUESDAY

Cucumber Carpaccio
with Mint Quinoa Salad

WEDNESDAY

Swiss Chard Frittata
with Spicy Pinto Beans

THURSDAY

Asian Noodle Soup

FRIDAY

Radish-Butter Flatbread
with Steamed Artichokes

SHOPPING LIST

Vegetables/Fruit

2 medium onions
1 bunch fresh flat-leaf parsley
1 bunch fresh mint
2 medium cucumbers
2 bunches red radishes (16 to 20)
1 bunch Swiss chard
One 3-inch piece of fresh ginger
2 fresh red Thai chile peppers or small red chiles or serranos
4 cups snow peas
4 artichokes
2 limes
1 lemon

Dairy

6 large eggs
3 Tablespoons unsalted butter
¼ cup grated Parmesan cheese
¼ cup crumbled feta cheese

Bakery/Misc.

Three 15-ounce cans pinto beans
4 ounces thin rice noodles (rice noodles are available in the Asian section of the grocery store)
4 whole wheat pitas
3¼ cups red quinoa (see Resources for where to buy)
1 Tablespoon sesame oil
1 Tablespoon rice wine vinegar

From the Pantry

1¾ teaspoons kosher salt
1¼ teaspoons black pepper
¾ teaspoon cayenne pepper
3 Tablespoons grapeseed oil
3 Tablespoons olive oil
5 garlic cloves
1 Tablespoon plus 1 teaspoon white wine vinegar
7 cups low-sodium vegetable broth
2 Tablespoons reduced-sodium soy sauce
¼ cup Pantry Dressing

PREP AHEAD

Quinoa for Monday and Tuesday

Prepare 8 cups quinoa (see page xvii).

Spring Week III: Monday

RED BEANS AND QUINOA

Red beans and rice is a traditional Creole dish, usually served on Mondays using Sunday's leftover ham or other meat. When I was growing up, a pot was often simmering at family gatherings. This vegetarian version uses quinoa instead of ham as a protein source. It's heart healthy but still has the satisfying feeling of that childhood meal.

Serves 4: 20 minutes   

2 Tablespoons grapeseed oil

1 medium onion, chopped

2 garlic cloves, minced or pressed

½ teaspoon kosher salt

¼ teaspoon cayenne pepper

Two 15-ounce cans pinto beans in liquid

1 teaspoon white wine vinegar

4 cups prepared red quinoa

¼ cup water

½ teaspoon black pepper

¼ cup chopped fresh flat-leaf parsley

Note: Canned beans are perfectly fine, but see for yourself how simple it is to prepare beans in the sidebar on page 39.

1. Heat the grapeseed oil in a large sauté pan over medium-high heat. Add the onion and garlic and cook until the onions soften, 4 to 5 minutes. Season with the salt and cayenne.

2. Add the beans and vinegar and bring to a simmer.

3. Meanwhile, in a medium saucepan, combine the quinoa, water, and pepper and heat over low heat.

4. Fold the parsley into the beans and serve over the quinoa.

beans

Loaded with protein, nutrients, and fiber, beans are a staple on The Fresh 20 menus. I try to use as many different varieties as possible throughout the year. Easily accessible at most markets and usually quite cheap, they are a simple solution for an everyday side dish or as a vegetarian protein. Keeping your pantry stocked with a variety of beans gives you a lot of options for dinner in a pinch. The Fresh 20 recipes often use black beans, pinto beans, garbanzo beans (chickpeas), and cannellini beans (white beans), but there is a multitude of choices on the grocery shelf—don't be afraid to try something new.

If you want to purchase dried beans, it's a good idea to prep them on the weekend, because they take a bit more time than canned. It's important to give the beans a good rinse and sort through them to make sure there are no rocks or dirt. On weeknights when time doesn't allow for soaking and cooking beans, I suggest using canned organic low-sodium beans.

Cooking Beans

I don't season beans until I am adding them to a meal, so this is a basic recipe that can be used to cook in bulk. Beans freeze well once cooked, so I usually double or triple the batch.

1 cup beans (pinto, black, cannellini, or kidney)

4 cups water (or broth)

1. Rinse the beans.

2. In a medium stockpot, add the beans and enough water to cover and soak the beans overnight.

3. Drain and rinse the beans. Add 4 cups of water or broth to cover the beans.

4. Bring to a boil, reduce the heat, and simmer for 90 minutes.

Yield: 1 cup dried beans makes 2 cups prepared

Cooked beans can be stored up to 1 week in the refrigerator and up to 6 months in the freezer.

CUCUMBER CARPACCIO

with Mint Quinoa Salad

Sometimes eating fresh means keeping ingredients close to their natural state. This elegant salad is a showstopper, sure to impress friends and family with its looks and flavor. Red quinoa is a colorful addition to the plate and delicious paired with fresh mint, but it may be harder to find. Regular quinoa works just as well.

Serves 4: 20 minutes   

for the cucumber carpaccio

2 Tablespoons olive oil

1 Tablespoon fresh lime juice

1 Tablespoon white wine vinegar

½ teaspoon kosher salt

2 medium cucumbers, sliced paper thin

4 red radishes, trimmed and sliced paper thin

½ teaspoon black pepper

¼ cup chopped fresh flat-leaf parsley

for the mint quinoa salad

½ cup low-sodium vegetable broth

¼ medium onion, finely chopped

4 cups prepared red quinoa

¼ cup finely chopped fresh mint

for the cucumber carpaccio

1. Whisk together the oil, lime juice, white wine vinegar, and salt in a large bowl.
2. Toss the cucumbers in the dressing. Arrange the cucumbers on a large platter.
3. Scatter the radishes over the cucumbers and season with the pepper.
4. Finish with a sprinkle of the parsley.

for the mint quinoa salad

1. Heat the broth in a medium saucepan over medium heat. Add the onion and cook for 3 to 4 minutes, or until softened.
2. Stir in the quinoa and heat until warmed through. Remove from the heat and fold in the mint.

a fresh idea

Plant an indoor herb garden in the spring to enjoy in the summer. Basil and thyme are simple to grow in small pots. Find small plants (seedlings) at your local nursery or start with organic seeds available in most hardware stores. Have each family member pick a different herb and have a race to track their growth.

Spring Week III: Wednesday

SWISS CHARD FRITTATA

with Spicy Pinto Beans

There's no reason to wait until Sunday brunch to enjoy a skillet frittata. Earthy Swiss chard sautéed in onions then combined with eggs and topped with Parmesan makes any weeknight special. Any leafy green can be substituted and adding your favorite vegetables is encouraged.

Serves 4: 30 minutes  

for the swiss chard frittata

1 Tablespoon olive oil

1 Tablespoon unsalted butter

¼ medium onion, finely chopped

1 garlic clove, minced or pressed

½ bunch Swiss chard, trimmed and finely chopped

½ cup low-sodium vegetable broth

6 large eggs

2 Tablespoons water

½ teaspoon kosher salt

¼ teaspoon black pepper

¼ cup grated Parmesan cheese

for the spicy pinto beans

One 15-ounce can pinto beans in liquid

½ teaspoon cayenne pepper

2 Tablespoons chopped fresh flat-leaf parsley

for the swiss chard frittata

1. Place a rack 6 inches from the heat and preheat the broiler.
2. Heat the olive oil and butter in a large ovenproof skillet over medium heat. Add the onion and garlic and sauté for 3 to 4 minutes. Add the chard and broth, bring to a simmer, and cook, stirring once or twice, until the chard leaves are just wilted, 3 to 5 minutes more.
3. Meanwhile, in a medium bowl, beat the eggs with the water until frothy. Add the salt and pepper.
4. Pour the egg mixture into the skillet and move the chard around to make sure the eggs cover the entire bottom of the pan. If desired, sprinkle the cheese on top. Cook the eggs until the bottom of the frittata is firm, about 5 minutes.
5. Transfer the pan to the broiler and broil until the top of the frittata has set and browned slightly.

for the spicy pinto beans

1. Mix the beans, cayenne, and parsley in a medium saucepan or bowl and heat over medium heat for about 2 minutes on the stovetop or in the microwave.
2. Serve the beans alongside the frittata.

ASIAN NOODLE SOUP

When I realized how simple this soup was to prepare at home, I was embarrassed at how many times I have ordered it in bulk from the local Chinese restaurant to feed my family. This homemade version allows you to control the amount of salt and to use the freshest vegetables.

Serves 4: 15 minutes   

- 1 Tablespoon grapeseed oil
- 1 Tablespoon sesame oil
- 2 garlic cloves, minced or pressed
- 1 Tablespoon minced fresh ginger
- 2 fresh red Thai chile peppers or small red chiles or serranos
- ½ medium onion, sliced
- ½ bunch Swiss chard, stems removed, chopped
- 6 cups low-sodium vegetable broth
- 4 ounces thin rice noodles
- 2 Tablespoons reduced-sodium soy sauce
- 2 cups snow peas
- 1 Tablespoon rice wine vinegar
- ¼ cup coarsely chopped fresh mint leaves
- 1 lime, cut in wedges
- 1 Tablespoon chopped fresh flat-leaf parsley

1. Heat the grapeseed and sesame oil in a large pot over medium-high heat. Add the garlic, ginger, and chile peppers and sauté until fragrant, about 1 minute. Remove the chile peppers if anyone is sensitive to hot food.

2. Add the onion and chard and cook until softened, about 4 minutes.

3. Pour in the broth and bring to a simmer. Add the noodles and soy sauce, stir to combine, and cook for 3 to 4 minutes, until the noodles are soft.

4. Remove from the heat and stir in the snow peas, rice wine vinegar, and mint.

5. Serve the soup with the lime wedges and parsley on the side.

Spring Week III: Thursday

Spring Week III: Friday

RADISH-BUTTER FLATBREAD

with Steamed Artichokes

Radishes do not get the attention they deserve, but they pack tons of flavor in a very small package. Most people use them raw in crudités or as a garnish for salad, but here they take center stage when they are transformed into a butter. When cooked, radishes mellow to a subtle, tangy, and entirely satisfying flavor.

for the radish butter

12 to 16 red radishes

2 Tablespoons unsalted butter, at room temperature

¼ teaspoon kosher salt

for the flatbread

4 whole wheat pitas, split into 8 thin rounds

¼ cup crumbled feta cheese

2 cups snow peas, cut in half

¼ cup fresh mint leaves

for the steamed artichokes

4 artichokes, stems cut away

Juice of 1 lemon

¼ cup Pantry Dressing of your choice (pages 26–7)

for the radish butter

1. Preheat the oven to 375°F.
2. Bring 4 cups of water to a boil in a medium saucepan. Add all but 2 radishes and boil for 10 minutes. Thinly slice remaining 2 radishes.
3. Drain the radishes and place in a food processor or blender. Pulse to puree, then add the butter and salt and pulse to blend.

For the flatbread

1. Put the pita rounds on a baking sheet and toast in the oven until crispy, about 5 minutes.
2. Spread a layer of the radish butter over each piece of pita, followed by a sprinkle of the feta cheese, a layer of the peas, and the sliced radishes. Garnish with the mint.

for the steamed artichokes

1. Cut away 1 inch from the top of each artichoke to expose the internal leaves. Trim the stem to the base.
2. Fill a large pot with a steamer insert with 3 inches of water, add the lemon juice, and bring to a simmer. Arrange the artichokes leaves down in the steamer, cover, and cook for 25 minutes, or until a leaf pulls away easily and the white flesh at the base of the leaves is tender.
3. Serve the artichokes with the dressing for dipping.

"IT HAS TRANSFORMED OUR WHOLE FAMILY."
—Samantha

Q: Why The Fresh 20?

A: By the time I found The Fresh 20 I had been on a personal quest to get my whole family into healthy shape for about six months. I had subscribed to and tried two other meal-planning services, but I was disappointed in the amount of processed foods that were being used, so I went on a search for one that didn't use processed foods. I saw The Fresh 20 and it was the answer I had been looking for! I subscribed immediately and have used it ever since.

Q: What were your family's eating habits like before joining The Fresh 20?

A: My husband, Casey, and I have three-year-old identical twin girls. When we joined The Fresh 20, the girls had just turned two. Since the day they were born, I vowed that they would get the healthiest start possible. I made all of their baby food, and they were used to eating all kinds of healthy snacks and fresh fruits and vegetables that I was not feeding to myself or to my husband. I would feed them the healthiest food possible and then, out of pure exhaustion and laziness, we would eat our meals from a drive-through after the girls went to bed.

When my girls turned two and I realized I had lost very little of the sixty pounds that I gained while pregnant, I knew things had to change once and for all. Since subscribing, I have changed all of my diet and exercise habits. I have lost more than forty pounds overall since last year and it has transformed our whole family. We eat together as a family every single night and I feel very good about the choices that I'm making for all of us when it comes to what we're eating. Plus, I feel as if I can really consider myself a healthy role model for my girls, which they deserve more than anything.

Q: Is The Fresh 20 helping your family create kitchen memories?

A: One of the best Mother's Day gifts that I got from my husband was a fancy apron for me plus two matching aprons for my girls. They love to wear them and they help me in the kitchen every day. They have been standing at the island counter with me for as long as they could stand up on a chair. They help me crack eggs, pour in things, measure spices, mix, and count veggies. Most of my best memories involve the kitchen or something we made together.

Q: How has The Fresh 20 changed your family?

A: It has seriously transformed our whole life. I knew I wanted us to all be as healthy as possible and that I had to eliminate all the processed foods from our diets. I wanted to make sure that my girls grew up in a house where our family eats one meal together every day and I wanted that meal to be good! I didn't know how to do it exactly, but The Fresh 20 took all the guesswork out of it for me. It gave me the ability to reach my personal health goals of losing weight on top of raising twins and working a full-time job from home. I couldn't be more grateful.

casey and samantha with daughters taylor and madden

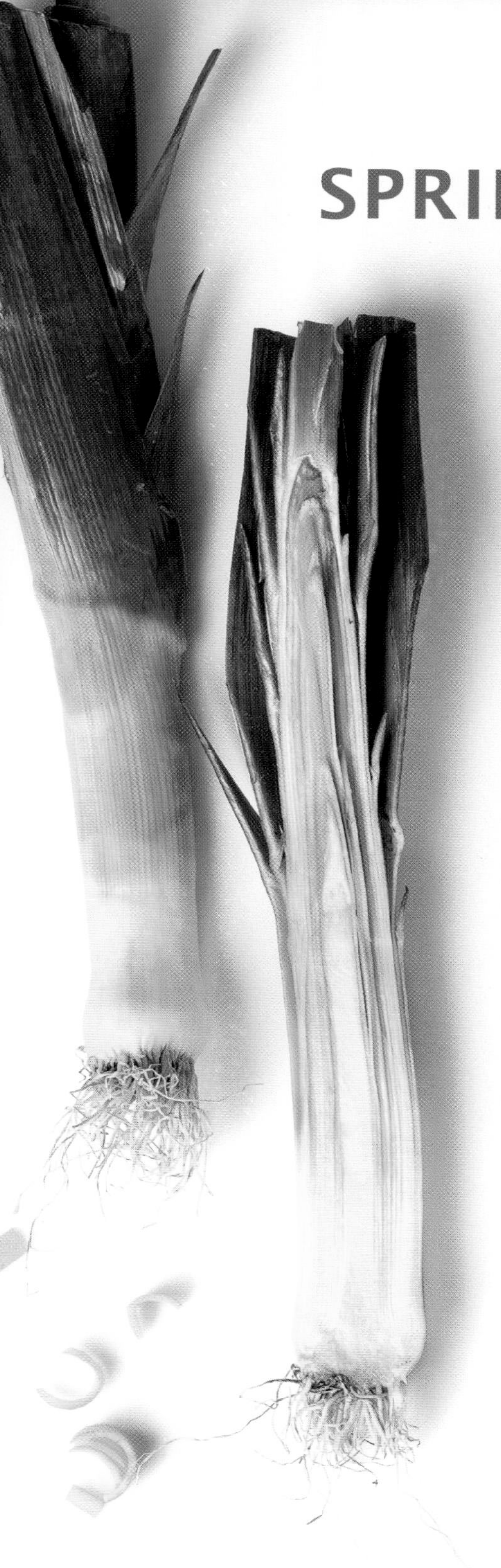

SPRING MENU

MONDAY

Pork Chops
with Crispy Kale and Farro

TUESDAY

Balsamic-Poached Salmon
with Asparagus and Couscous

WEDNESDAY

Skirt Steak
with Goat Cheese
and Couscous Kale Salad

THURSDAY

Apple and Leek Soup
with Pork Quesadillas

FRIDAY

Spinach Strata

SHOPPING LIST

Meat/Seafood

6 bone-in pork chops
4 skin-on salmon fillets (about 5 ounces each)
1½ pounds skirt steak

Vegetables/Fruit

1 medium onion
2 leeks
4 bunches kale
1 pound asparagus
4 cups baby spinach
2 lemons
4 Granny Smith apples

Dairy

8 large eggs
1 cup grated white cheddar cheese
5 ounces goat cheese

Bakery/Misc.

4 whole wheat tortillas
2 whole wheat bakery rolls
1 cup farro
2 cups couscous

From the Pantry

5¼ teaspoons kosher salt
2 teaspoons black pepper
½ teaspoon sweet Hungarian paprika
2 teaspoons dried oregano
1 teaspoon grapeseed oil
9 Tablespoons plus ¼ cup olive oil
4 garlic cloves
½ cup balsamic vinegar
6 cups low-sodium chicken or vegetable broth
1 teaspoon Dijon mustard
1 Tablespoon The Fresh 20 Spice Blend (page xxii)

Spring Week IV: Monday

PORK CHOPS

with Crispy Kale and Farro

For the longest time, I disliked pork chops because they always turned out overdone. I started to undercook them a little and wrap them in foil to finish cooking. Voilà! Perfectly moist and juicy every time. Here, I paired them with farro, a super grain loaded with nutrition. Brown rice or quinoa can be substituted.

Serves 4: 20 minutes 

for the farro

1 cup farro

2 cups water

Pinch of kosher salt

for the pork chops

6 bone-in pork chops

1 teaspoon kosher salt

½ teaspoon black pepper

½ teaspoon sweet Hungarian paprika

2 teaspoons dried oregano

for the crispy kale

¼ cup olive oil

2 bunches kale, stems removed, chopped

2 garlic cloves, minced or pressed

¼ teaspoon kosher salt

¼ teaspoon black pepper

Juice of ½ lemon

for the farro

Combine the farro, water, and salt in a medium saucepan, cover, and bring the water to a boil over medium-high heat. Reduce the heat to a low simmer and cook for 30 minutes, or until the farro is softened but still a little crunchy.

for the pork chops

1. Preheat an outdoor grill to medium-high heat.
2. Season the pork chops on both sides with the salt, pepper, paprika, and oregano. Grill the chops for 3 to 4 minutes per side, until no longer pink in the middle. Remove from the heat.
3. Wrap the chops in foil and let sit for 5 to 7 minutes to complete cooking.

Leftover Note: Store 2 of the chops in an airtight container in the refrigerator for dinner on Thursday.

for the crispy kale

1. Heat a large nonstick sauté pan over medium-high heat. Add the oil. Once the oil is hot, add the kale and garlic and sauté over high heat until the kale begins to brown lightly around the edges and turn crispy.
2. Season the kale with the salt and pepper, drizzle the lemon juice over the top, and remove from the heat.

BALSAMIC-POACHED SALMON

with Asparagus and Couscous

Poaching is an underused cooking technique. It's a great way to cook without oil and a gentle method to prepare delicate fish. Here the balsamic vinegar infuses the salmon with a sweet and tangy hint of flavor. Asparagus has always been a nice companion to salmon. If it ain't broke . . .

Serves 4: 30 minutes

for the couscous

2 cups low-sodium chicken or vegetable broth

2 cups couscous

2 Tablespoons olive oil

Juice of ½ lemon

¼ teaspoon black pepper

for the asparagus

1 pound asparagus, tough ends trimmed

1 Tablespoon olive oil

½ teaspoon kosher salt

¼ teaspoon black pepper

for the balsamic-poached salmon

2 cups low-sodium chicken or vegetable broth

½ cup balsamic vinegar

1 teaspoon kosher salt

¼ teaspoon black pepper

4 skin-on salmon fillets (about 5 ounces each)

for the couscous

1. In a medium saucepan, bring the broth to a boil over medium-high heat. Stir in the couscous, cover, and turn off the heat. Allow the couscous to stand for 20 minutes.
2. Add the olive oil, lemon juice, and pepper to the couscous and stir to combine.

Leftover Note: Store half of the couscous in an airtight container in the refrigerator for dinner on Wednesday.

for the asparagus

1. Place a rack in the top third of the oven and preheat the oven to 450°F. Line a baking sheet with parchment paper.
2. Put the asparagus on the baking sheet and toss with the olive oil, salt, and pepper. Spread the asparagus out and roast for 10 minutes.
3. Serve the warm asparagus over the couscous.

for the balsamic-poached salmon

1. Combine the broth, balsamic vinegar, salt, and pepper in a large 2- to 3-inch-deep sauté pan and bring to a boil over medium-high heat.
2. Add the fish, skin side down, and reduce the heat to a low simmer. Cover and cook the fish for 5 minutes, then remove from the poaching liquid to serve.

Spring Week IV: Tuesday

Spring Week IV: Wednesday

SKIRT STEAK

with Goat Cheese and Couscous Kale Salad

A grain, a green, and a cheese walk into a bar. Bartender says, "Yum." Jokes aside, this dinner is about simple ingredients coming together to deliver huge flavors in very little time. And, yes, I know I'll never be a comedian.

Serves 4: 15 minutes

for the skirt steak

1 Tablespoon The Fresh 20 Spice Blend (page xxii)

¾ teaspoon kosher salt

1½ pounds skirt steak

2 Tablespoons olive oil

for the goat cheese and couscous kale salad

2 cups leftover couscous (see Tuesday, page 54)

2 bunches kale, stems removed, chopped into small bite-sized pieces

2 ounces goat cheese, crumbled

Grated zest and juice of 1 lemon

1 Tablespoon olive oil

Kosher salt and black pepper

for the skirt steak

1. Combine the spice blend with salt. Season both sides of the skirt steak with the seasoning.
2. Heat a large nonstick sauté pan or grill pan over medium-high heat. Add the oil, and once it is hot, add the meat and cook for 2 to 3 minutes per side for rare, or to the desired doneness. Let the meat rest before slicing it against the grain.

for the goat cheese and couscous kale salad

1. In a medium bowl, fluff the couscous with a fork.
2. Toss in the chopped kale, goat cheese, lemon zest and juice, olive oil, and salt and pepper to taste and mix well.

APPLE AND LEEK SOUP

with Pork Quesadillas

Apples in spring may seem off, but there are still some varieties at the market that hold up well in soups and offer up sweetness, like the Granny Smiths used in this recipe. Quesadillas are the perfect companion to soup.

Serves 4: 35 minutes

for the apple and leek soup

- 2 leeks, root ends trimmed
- 2 Tablespoons olive oil
- 1 medium onion, coarsely chopped
- 2 Granny Smith apples, peeled, cored, and diced
- 1 garlic clove, minced or pressed
- 2 cups low-sodium chicken or vegetable broth
- 2 cups water
- 1 teaspoon kosher salt
- ¼ teaspoon black pepper

for the pork quesadillas

- 2 leftover pork chops (see Monday, page 53), meat removed from the bone and cut into thin slices
- 1 teaspoon grapeseed oil
- 4 whole wheat tortillas
- 1 cup grated white cheddar cheese

for the apple and leek soup

1. Cut the leeks lengthwise in half and wash thoroughly to remove any dirt. Drain and pat dry, then coarsely chop.

2. Heat the oil in a 4-quart Dutch oven or other heavy pot over medium-high heat. Add the leeks, onion, apples, and garlic and cook, stirring occasionally, until the vegetables begin to soften, about 4 minutes. If desired, remove and reserve ¼ cup of the sautéed leeks, onions, and apples for the soup garnish.

3. Add the broth, water, salt, and pepper, bring to a gentle simmer, and cook for 20 minutes, until softened.

4. Puree the soup in batches in a blender or food processor until smooth. Serve warm.

for the pork quesadillas

1. Heat a small sauté pan over medium-high heat. Warm the pork chop slices, then remove from the pan and set aside.

2. Lightly brush the pan with the oil.

3. Warm the tortillas on both sides. Spread ¼ cup of the cheese over half of each tortilla, followed by one-quarter of the pork slices. Fold the tortillas over and warm in the pan until the cheese is melted.

4. Cut the tortillas in half and serve warm with the soup.

Spring Week IV:
Thursday

Spring Week IV: Friday

SPINACH STRATA

By the end of the week, bread starts to stale. I seize the opportunity to prepare this comfort-food dish. Spinach makes the simple strata a nutritious meal. Goat cheese seals the deal with its nutty essence and its smooth texture against the crunch of the bread cubes. Let the rolls stand out overnight before cubing it; they're better stale.

Serves 5: 50 minutes

- 1 teaspoon olive oil
- 1 teaspoon Dijon mustard
- 1 garlic clove, minced or pressed
- 8 large eggs
- ¾ teaspoon kosher salt
- ¼ teaspoon black pepper
- 4 cups baby spinach
- 2 whole wheat bakery rolls, cubed (about 2 cups)
- 3 ounces goat cheese, crumbled
- 2 Granny Smith apples, cored and cut into wedges

1. Preheat the oven to 350°F.
2. In a medium bowl, combine the olive oil, Dijon mustard, garlic, eggs, salt, and pepper and whisk until completely blended and slightly frothy.
3. Lightly grease a small deep casserole dish. Arrange the spinach in an even layer in the bottom of the dish, followed by the bread cubes and goat cheese.
4. Pour the egg mixture over the bread and bake for 35 to 40 minutes, or until the eggs have completely set.
5. Serve with a side of the apples.

IN SEASON

- Arugula
- Avocados
- Basil
- Bell peppers
- Blueberries
- Butter lettuce
- Corn
- Cucumbers
- Green beans
- Limes
- Mint
- Radishes
- Strawberries
- Tomatoes
- Watermelon
- Zucchini

SUMMER

Summer is for children, and every cook has an inner child. The school year is over and it is time to have fun. This is the season when most ingredients don't need a cook as a handler—they can speak for themselves. Fruits and vegetables are bursting with flavor. Bring on the tomatoes! Oh, those fat red beefsteak tomatoes! My summer memories include watering down the backyard Slip 'N Slide with the garden hose and slurping up the cherry Popsicles that followed. We dunked them in fresh lemonade until the liquid turned pink. Dad was at the barbecue, basting ribs and grilling the best Midwest yellow corn a quarter could buy. No butter necessary. There were summers that I lived on tomatoes, cherry Popsicles, and corn alone.

The Fresh 20 summer weeknight dinners use the grill to make quick work of seasonal ingredients. Make-ahead dressings, pestos, and marinades help boost the flavor, and spare you any lingering over a hot stove. No other season gives us so much for so little effort.

The farmers' markets explode with choices and great value. My family makes trips to the market a weekly outing; we can't get enough of summer fruit. And then there is the garden. I grow my own tomatoes, and the anticipation builds from "opening day"—early May, when the Green Zebra seedlings go in the ground—until the All-Stars begin to emerge. Arriving home from the market on Saturdays in July and August, I try to outrace my boys, husband included, to get to the tomato plants first. Our tomatoes never make it as far as the dinner table. Green Zebra theft is our family's summer game.

It's time to head outside, soak up the sunshine, and spend time with family. Enjoy the most bountiful season of fresh food.

SUMMER MENU

MONDAY

Strawberry Gazpacho
with Feta Cheese Crostini

TUESDAY

Panfried Chicken Milanese
with Arugula Salad

WEDNESDAY

Mediterranean Mezze Plate

THURSDAY

Tabbouleh
with Grilled Sausages

FRIDAY

Vegetarian Niçoise Salad

SHOPPING LIST

Meat/Seafood

4 fresh Italian sausage links (any variety)

2 boneless, skinless organic chicken breasts (about 1¼ pounds)

Vegetables/Fruit

3 pounds medium ripe tomatoes, plus 2 tomatoes

12 ounces cherry or grape tomatoes (about 2 cups)

2 medium cucumbers

3 red bell peppers

1 medium red onion

1 pint fresh strawberries

4 cups baby arugula

5 lemons

1 large Japanese eggplant

2 bunches fresh flat-leaf parsley

1 romaine lettuce heart

8 ounces green beans

8 baby Yukon Gold or fingerling potatoes

Dairy

4 large eggs

8 ounces feta cheese

Bakery/Misc.

6 whole wheat pitas

1 cup sesame seeds

Two 15-ounce cans chickpeas (garbanzo beans)

1 cup bulgur wheat

From the Pantry

3¾ teaspoons kosher salt

1 teaspoon black pepper

¾ teaspoon sweet Hungarian paprika

1 Tablespoon white wine vinegar

5 garlic cloves

1½ cups olive oil

2 cups low-sodium chicken or vegetable broth

½ cup Pantry Dressing of your choice (pages 26–7)

PREP AHEAD

Roasted Red Peppers for Wednesday

2 red bell peppers

1. Preheat the outdoor grill.
2. Lay the whole red peppers on the grill and char, turning occasionally, until blackened on all sides, about 10 minutes. Transfer to a paper lunch bag or gallon-sized Ziploc bag and let rest for 5 minutes, or until cool enough to touch.
3. With your fingers, peel away and discard the burned skin. Remove the stems of the peppers. Scoop out the seeds, being careful to reserve as much liquid as possible. Cut the peppers into strips and transfer to a bowl, along with their juice. Store in airtight container.

grilling indoors

The heat of summer entices us all to take the cooking outside. Many summer recipes use the grill, but they will work inside on the stovetop as well. A grill pan is best, but a large dry skillet will work in a pinch.

Oven Alternative

Preheat the oven to 400°F. Pull the meat out of the refrigerator and bring to room temperature, about 15 minutes. Dry the meat by blotting lightly with a paper towel. Heat a large nonstick ovenproof sauté pan over medium-high heat and brush with 1 Tablespoon of grapeseed oil. Sear the meat about 2 minutes per side until golden brown. Place into the oven and bake twice the amount of time indicated for grilling. Remove from the oven and cover with foil, and allow to rest for an additional 5 minutes.

Stovetop Grill Pan

Take the meat out of the refrigerator and bring to room temperature, about 15 minutes. Dry the meat by blotting lightly with a paper towel. Heat a large grill pan over medium-high heat and brush with 1 Tablespoon of grapeseed oil. Arrange the meat in the grill pan and sear the meat on both sides until golden brown. Reduce the heat to medium-low and continue cooking until desired doneness. Flip as necessary to evenly cook on both sides.

Tahini for Wednesday

1 cup sesame seeds

⅓ cup olive oil

1. Heat a sauté pan over medium-high heat. Add the sesame seeds and toast lightly, about 2 minutes, shaking the pan to prevent burning. Remove from the heat and let cool.

2. Add the toasted sesame seeds to a food processor or blender, pour in the olive oil, and pulse on high for 2 to 4 minutes, until the tahini is somewhat smooth. Scrape the tahini into an airtight container and store in the refrigerator for up to 2 weeks.

Baba Ganoush for Wednesday

1 Tablespoon olive oil

1 large Japanese eggplant, ends trimmed

1 garlic clove, minced or pressed

¼ teaspoon kosher salt

¼ bunch fresh flat-leaf parsley, finely chopped, long stems removed

2 Tablespoons tahini (from above)

2 Tablespoons fresh lemon juice

1. Preheat an outdoor grill. Brush the grill with the olive oil to prevent sticking.

2. Grill the eggplant whole, turning occasionally, for 10 to 15 minutes. If the skin gets a little burned, it is perfectly fine. Let the eggplant cool.

3. Cut the eggplant lengthwise in half. Scoop the flesh into a food processor and puree until smooth. Add the garlic, salt, parsley, and tahini and pulse to combine. Add the lemon juice a teaspoon at a time, tasting after each addition, until the desired tang is achieved. Transfer to a serving bowl. Refrigerate until ready to serve.

Hardboiled Eggs for Friday

4 large eggs

1. Place the eggs in a small pot and cover with water by 1 inch.

2. Bring the water to a boil. Cover and then take off the heat.

3. Let the eggs sit for 10 minutes. Peel the eggs and store in the refrigerator.

STRAWBERRY GAZPACHO

with Feta Cheese Crostini

Traditional tomato and cucumber gazpacho, which originated in Spain, is a great quencher on a hot day. Here strawberries add another layer of flavor. Some people like their gazpacho chunky, others like it smooth—adjust it to suit your taste. Don't be tempted to add more red onion, as it can overpower the soup. I love the way the creamy feta cheese complements the sweet acidity of the gazpacho.

For fun, serve in teacups and sit outside on the patio on a hot evening, sipping away.

Serves 4: 25 minutes 

for the strawberry gazpacho

3 pounds medium ripe tomatoes, cored

1 medium cucumber, peeled

1 medium red bell pepper, cored and seeded

¼ medium red onion

2 garlic cloves

½ bunch fresh flat-leaf parsley, long stems removed

1 pint fresh strawberries, hulled

Juice of 1 lemon, or to taste

1 Tablespoon white wine vinegar, or to taste

1 teaspoon kosher salt, or to taste

Up to ½ cup water, if desired

1 Tablespoon olive oil

for the feta cheese crostini

2 whole wheat pitas, cut into quarters

1 Tablespoon olive oil

¼ teaspoon black pepper

3 ounces feta cheese, crumbled

for the strawberry gazpacho

1. In batches, combine the tomatoes, cucumber, bell pepper, red onion, garlic, parsley, and strawberries in a blender or food processor and puree until relatively smooth; for a chunky version, pulse instead of puree.
2. Add half of the lemon juice, vinegar, and salt and blend. Taste and adjust the seasoning as necessary by adding lemon juice, vinegar, and/or salt. If the gazpacho is too thick, add some or all of the water. Refrigerate for at least 10 minutes.
3. Transfer the gazpacho to a large bowl. Drizzle with the olive oil.
4. Serve in bowls, teacups, or glasses.

for the feta cheese crostini

1. Toast the pitas under the broiler or in a toaster oven until slightly crispy.
2. Combine the olive oil, pepper, and feta cheese in a bowl, mixing until smooth.
3. Spread the cheese on the pita triangles.

 omit the crostini  omit the feta

Summer Week I: Monday

Summer Week I: Tuesday

PANFRIED CHICKEN MILANESE

with Arugula Salad

Fried chicken is an American classic. This is a satisfying variation—lighter, full of flavor, and made with much less oil. The key is getting the chicken breasts very thin and even. That can be tricky, but it's worth the effort. If you don't have a meat mallet, a rolling pin and some muscle will do just fine.

Serves 4: 25 minutes 

for the chicken milanese

2 boneless, skinless organic chicken breasts, sliced lengthwise into 4 thin pieces

½ teaspoon kosher salt

½ teaspoon black pepper

½ teaspoon sweet Hungarian paprika

¼ cup olive oil

for the arugula salad

4 cups baby arugula, washed and dried

6 ounces cherry or grape tomatoes (about 1 cup)

¼ cup dressing of your choice (see Pantry Dressings, pages 26–7)

2 ounces feta cheese, crumbled

for the chicken milanese

1. One at a time, place each piece of chicken between two pieces of parchment paper or plastic wrap and pound to ⅛ inch thick. Season the chicken on both sides with the salt, pepper, and paprika.

2. Heat the olive oil in a 12-inch skillet until very hot. Add the chicken cutlets, being careful not to crowd the pan (it may be necessary to cook the chicken in batches), and cook for about 4 minutes per side, or until golden brown on both sides. Remove from the heat and transfer to a paper-towel-lined plate.

for the arugula salad

1. In a bowl, toss the arugula and tomatoes with the dressing.

2. Top each chicken piece with about a cup of the arugula salad. Sprinkle with the feta cheese.

MEDITERRANEAN MEZZE PLATE

Salad platters are the perfect way to keep dinner simple during the busy summer months. Hummus is the star of this plate. For ease, use canned chickpeas, which, in my opinion, are completely acceptable for something you are going to puree anyway. This light meal is perfect for entertaining.

Serves 6 

for the hummus

Two 15-ounce cans chickpeas, drained and rinsed

½ cup olive oil, plus more for drizzling

Juice of 1 lemon

2 garlic cloves

1½ teaspoons kosher salt

1 Tablespoon Tahini (see Prep Ahead, page 67)

¼ teaspoon black pepper

2 Tablespoons chopped fresh flat-leaf parsley

¼ teaspoon sweet Hungarian paprika

for the platter

Baba Ganoush (see Prep Ahead, page 67)

Roasted Red Peppers (see Prep Ahead, page 66)

½ cup tahini (see Prep Ahead, page 67)

3 ounces feta cheese, chopped or crumbled

4 whole wheat pitas, toasted and cut into wedges

1 medium cucumber, peeled and cut into rounds

for the hummus

1. In a blender, combine all the ingredients except the parsley and paprika and pulse on high speed for 30 seconds. Scrape down the sides of the bowl and puree until smooth. Adjust the consistency and thickness to the desired level by adding the oil a little at a time.

2. Scrape the hummus onto a plate or into a bowl. Sprinkle with the parsley and paprika. Cover with plastic wrap and set aside.

3. Just before serving, drizzle a bit of olive oil over the top of the hummus.

to serve

Set out the bowls of hummus, baba ganoush, tahini, roasted red peppers, and feta cheese, along with the pitas and cucumbers for dipping or scooping.

omit pita and serve with cut veggies

omit feta

Summer Week I:
Wednesday

Summer Week I:
Thursday

TABBOULEH

with Grilled Sausages

A traditional Middle Eastern mezze, this tabbouleh dish features bulgur wheat and fresh parsley. The salad is even better when made ahead, so toss it together in the morning and let the flavors meld. Grilled Italian sausage with fennel makes a great partner. I like my tabbouleh with a chilled glass of rosé wine, but only if someone else is doing the dishes.

Serves 4: 1 hour 

for the tabbouleh

- 2 cups low-sodium chicken or vegetable broth
- 1 cup quick-cooking bulgur wheat, such as Bob's Red Mill
- 2 Tablespoons olive oil
- Juice of 2 lemons
- 2 medium tomatoes, chopped
- ½ bunch fresh flat-leaf parsley, leaves finely chopped
- ¼ medium red onion, finely chopped
- ½ teaspoon kosher salt

for the sausages

- 4 fresh Italian sausage links (any variety)
- Serve with leftover hummus, baba ganoush, or roasted red peppers

for the tabbouleh

1. Bring the broth to a boil in a large saucepan. Pour in the bulgur, cover, remove from the heat, and let sit for 1 hour; drain.
2. Combine the bulgur, olive oil, and lemon juice in a large serving bowl. Mix in the tomato, parsley, and onion. Season with the salt.

Note: Tabbouleh is best when made ahead; at a minimum, let stand for a half hour before serving.

for the sausages

1. Preheat an outdoor grill.
2. Grill the sausages, turning occasionally, until cooked through.

V omit sausages

 use quinoa instead of bulgur

Summer Week I:
Friday

VEGETARIAN NIÇOISE SALAD

I never miss the traditional tuna in this composed salad. I skip the capers as well because, in my opinion, they add too much salt to a delicious display of summer's bounty. Have fun arranging the platter in a decorative pattern or design. It's a weeknight, but feel free to get fancy.

Serves 4: 20 minutes   

- 8 baby Yukon Gold or fingerling potatoes
- 8 ounces green beans
- 1 romaine lettuce heart, chopped
- 4 hard-boiled eggs, peeled and cut in half (see Prep Ahead, page 67)
- 6 ounces cherry or grape tomatoes (about 1 cup)
- ½ red onion, thinly sliced
- ¼ cup dressing of your choice (Pantry Dressing, pages 26–7)
- Freshly ground pepper

1. Place the potatoes in a pan and add enough water to cover the potatoes by half an inch. Bring the water to a boil and boil until fork-tender, 6 to 8 minutes depending on the heat.

2. Add the green beans and steam, 1 minute.

3. Drain, then rinse with cold water. Once cool, cut the potatoes in half.

4. Arrange the lettuce on a big serving platter. Arrange the green beans, potatoes, eggs, tomatoes, and red onion on top in a decorative pattern.

5. Season with freshly ground pepper and serve with the dressing on the side.

a fresh idea:

PREP HERBS

Remove the leaves from herbs as soon as you get home from the market. Make sure they are clean and dry, then wrap in a paper towel, slide them into a Ziploc bag, and store in the crisper. You will use them more often if they are at the ready. Trust me, this advance prep might feel like a chore, but at dinnertime, you'll be glad you did it.

SUMMER MENU WEEK 2

MONDAY
Spring Roll in a Bowl

TUESDAY
Salmon Salad Pitas
with Fresh Berries

WEDNESDAY
The Fresh 20 Turkey Burgers
with Carrot Slaw

THURSDAY
Polenta Pan Pizza

FRIDAY
Summer Smorgasbord
with Shredded Carrots

SHOPPING LIST

Meat/Seafood

1 pound ground turkey
12 ounces wild salmon fillet
4 ounces thinly sliced salami (from the deli)
4 ounces thinly sliced lean turkey breast (from the butcher)

Vegetables/Fruits

2 heads butter lettuce
3 bell peppers, 1 red, 1 yellow or orange, and 1 green
3 cucumbers
9 medium carrots
1 pound heirloom tomatoes, plus 1 medium tomato
6 ounces grape or cherry tomatoes (about 1 cup)
1 bunch fresh basil
2 lemons
½ red onion
1 pint fresh strawberries or berry of choice
2 ripe but firm avocados

Dairy

10 ounces mozzarella (from the deli)
8 slices provolone cheese (from the deli)

Bakery/Misc.

4 whole wheat pitas
5 whole wheat hamburger buns
4 ounces thin rice noodles (rice noodles are available in the Asian section of the grocery store)
1 cup quick-cooking polenta or cornmeal, medium grain

From the Pantry

2 teaspoons kosher salt
1¼ teaspoons black pepper
Pinch of cayenne pepper
3 teaspoons dried oregano
3 teaspoons herbes de Provence
2 Tablespoons grapeseed oil
3 Tablespoons olive oil
2 Tablespoons Dijon mustard
5 cups low-sodium chicken or vegetable broth
2 teaspoons white wine vinegar
2 Tablespoons honey
3 Tablespoons reduced-sodium soy sauce

PREP AHEAD

Soy Dressing for Monday

3 Tablespoons reduced-sodium soy sauce

2 teaspoons white wine vinegar

1 Tablespoon honey

¼ teaspoon black pepper

Pinch of cayenne pepper

In a small bowl, whisk together the soy sauce, vinegar, honey, black pepper, and cayenne. Store in an airtight container in the refrigerator for up to 5 days.

Yield: ¼ cup

Bread Crumbs for Wednesday

1 whole wheat hamburger bun

1. Split the bun in half, and toast until crispy, but not burned.

2. In a blender, grind the toasted bun until mealy in texture. Store in an airtight container in the refrigerator for up to a week.

Yield: ½ cup

a fresh idea:

CREATE MEMORIES

So many of my best memories involve meals with my family. Create happy kitchen moments: Make dinner the destination. Play cards after eating. Create word games. We play name games like "all the dogs you can think of" and "all the countries that start with *S*." Think of memories that make you happy and share them at the dinner table. It's the most wonderful place to have family conversations.

farmers' markets

The freshest produce, of course, comes right from the farm, but finding fresh ingredients is only one of many reasons to head to open-air markets. It's also a great time to learn about food and get preparation and storage advice from the source—the farmer and his team. Summer farmers' markets make great family outings. Many now have activities for kids, like the balloon man at the Hollywood Farmers' Market and the dancing vegetable people in the market at Union Square in New York City. The fun atmosphere makes the markets a great place to encourage children to taste new things—seize the moment! The only problem with the markets is resisting the abundance of choices. Try to remain aware of exactly what you will use and curb the temptation to load the car full of eye-catching colorful fruits and crisp vegetables. Too much food can quickly go to waste. Take a list, purchase with care, and enjoy the best of the season.

The Farmer Connection

The farmer is your best resource when it comes to choosing the freshest and tastiest produce. Knowing where your food comes from, who grows it, and how it is grown can help you make sustainable choices. Next time you are visiting the farmers' market, strike up a conversation.

This list of questions should help you get to know the farm and what it produces better.

How big is your farm?
What other crops do you grow?
How long will this be in season?
What's the best way to prepare it?
How do I choose the best produce?
Do you use organic methods?
What do you use for pest and weed control?
Do you belong to a co-op?
What's coming up in a few weeks this season?

Summer Week II: Monday

SPRING ROLL IN A BOWL

After wrestling with the traditional rice wrappers, I gave up and went for the simpler bowl method. The flavors are all still present, and everyone can build their own with the ingredients they most prefer. It's okay to be flexible with a recipe: when all else fails, keep it simple.

Serves 4: 20 minutes   

4 ounces thin rice noodles

2 medium carrots, peeled and cut into matchsticks

1 cucumber, peeled and cut into matchsticks

6 to 8 basil leaves, torn to pieces

¼ cup Soy Dressing (see Prep Ahead, page 80)

1 head butter lettuce, separated into leaves, washed, dried, and roughly chopped

2 ripe but firm avocados, halved, pitted, peeled, and cut into slices

1. Soak the rice noodles in warm water for 5 minutes until soft.

2. In a medium bowl, combine the rice noodles, carrots, and cucumber and toss with the basil and half of the soy dressing.

3. Divide the lettuce among four bowls and top with the dressed noodles.

4. Finish with the sliced avocado and serve with the remaining dressing on the side.

SALMON SALAD PITAS

with Fresh Berries

Served hot or cold, salmon is the perfect summer fish. Here it is tossed with a simple salad of cool cucumber and refreshing lemon and stuffed into warm pitas for a meal that is the essence of summer. Add a bowl of fresh berries to the mix, and you have conquered the heat!

Serves 4: 20 minutes 

2 cups low-sodium chicken or vegetable broth

Juice of 1 lemon

12 ounces wild salmon fillet

2 Tablespoons olive oil

Pinch of kosher salt

Pinch of black pepper

½ head butter lettuce, separated into leaves, washed, dried, and roughly chopped

1 medium carrot, peeled and shredded

¼ red onion, cut into thin slices

1 cucumber, peeled and cut into thin slices

2 whole wheat pitas, cut in half and warmed

1 pint fresh strawberries, washed and hulled, or berry of choice

1. Combine the broth and half of the lemon juice in a deep skillet and bring to a boil over medium heat. Reduce the heat to a simmer, add the salmon, and simmer over low heat for 5 minutes. Remove the salmon from the pan and set aside to cool; discard the broth.

2. In a small bowl, whisk together the remaining lemon juice, olive oil, salt, and pepper.

3. Break the salmon into chunks into a medium bowl.

4. Add the lettuce, carrot, red onion, and cucumber.

5. Add the dressing and toss the salad gently. Stuff the salad into the warm pitas.

4. Serve one pita half per person, with a side of the fresh strawberries or berry of your choice.

Summer Week II:
Tuesday

American family staples like ketchup are rarely made from scratch. It is too convenient and even economical to buy them. But homemade ketchup has two main benefits: You, not the manufacturer, are in control of the sugar and salt content. And the ketchup actually tastes like tomatoes, not some thick, salty mystery paste.

When I banished processed ingredients from my kitchen, I removed everything with corn syrup. I struggled to make a homemade version of ketchup that could stand up to my lingering childhood expectation—Heinz was the barometer. I love this version so much I'm tempted to learn how to make my own hot dogs.

Yield: 2 cups: 1 hour

- 2 Tablespoons olive oil
- 1 medium yellow onion, peeled and quartered
- 3 celery stalks, cut into 1-inch pieces
- 6 ounces tomato paste
- 3 pounds tomatoes, cored and quartered
- 2 Tablespoons pure maple syrup
- ½ cup white wine vinegar
- 1 teaspoon ground cumin
- 1 teaspoon kosher salt
- 1 teaspoon black pepper
- ½ teaspoon cayenne pepper
- Up to 1 cup water

1. Heat the olive oil in a 5-quart Dutch oven or other heavy pot over medium-high heat. Add the onion and celery and cook until tender, about 7 minutes.

2. Add the tomato paste, stirring to coat the onions. Add the tomatoes, maple syrup, white wine vinegar, and spices and bring to a boil. Cook for 15 minutes.

3. In a food processor or blender, puree the tomatoes for at least 20 seconds on medium, until smooth. Add water if necessary. Strain the liquid into a 2-quart saucepan, bring to a simmer over medium heat, and simmer the ketchup for 30 minutes, or until it starts to thicken. Transfer the ketchup to a jar and let cool. Seal the jar and store the ketchup in the refrigerator for up to a month.

Tips

- The quality of your ketchup is based on the quality of your ingredients.
- Let the onions and celery caramelize to deepen the flavor.
- The longer you simmer and reduce, the thicker your final product.
- Store the ketchup in several small containers that can be sealed until ready to use; 1-cup mason jars work perfectly!

No fresh tomatoes? Here's my quick pantry version:

⅓ cup water

½ onion, quartered

6 ounces tomato paste

1 garlic clove, whole

⅓ cup maple syrup

⅓ cup white wine vinegar

1 teaspoon kosher salt

1. Place all the ingredients in a blender and puree until smooth.

2. Transfer the liquid to a small pot and simmer for 15 minutes.

3. Stir and continue to simmer until the liquid has reduced and thickened.

Add-ins

- A simple teaspoon of a flavorful spice can change the flavor profile of the ketchup. Try curry powder, turmeric, or Chinese five-spice powder.

Serving Ideas

Baked fries are a no-brainer for ketchup, but have you tried it on . . .

- Baked potato
- Scrambled eggs
- Instead of mayo on a cold meatloaf sandwich
- Baked chicken nuggets
- Pasta (it's happened)

Summer Week II: Wednesday

THE FRESH 20 TURKEY BURGERS

with Carrot Slaw

As turkey burgers go, ours are pretty spectacular. I can say this because so many subscribers weighed in on the recipe. Juicy inside and stuffed with basil and provolone cheese, these are no ordinary burgers. Keep this recipe on summer long repeat.

Serves 4: 30 minutes

for the turkey burgers

1 pound ground turkey

½ cup Bread Crumbs (see Prep Ahead, page 80)

Juice of ½ lemon

½ green bell pepper, finely chopped

1 Tablespoon shredded fresh basil

2 teaspoons dried oregano

1 teaspoon kosher salt

½ teaspoon black pepper

4 thin slices provolone cheese

4 whole wheat hamburger buns, split and toasted

Pantry Dressing (pages 26–7) and/or ketchup, homemade (page 87) or organic store-bought

4 butter lettuce leaves

1 medium tomato, sliced

for the carrot slaw

Juice of ½ lemon

1 teaspoon herbes de Provence

1 Tablespoon honey

2 Tablespoons grapeseed oil

½ teaspoon kosher salt

¼ teaspoon black pepper

6 medium carrots, peeled and shredded

for the turkey burgers

1. Preheat an outdoor grill.
2. Combine the turkey, bread crumbs, lemon juice, green bell pepper, basil, oregano, salt, and pepper in a medium bowl and mix well.
3. Divide the turkey mixture into 8 equal portions and form into thin patties. Place 1 slice of the cheese on top of a turkey patty and place a second patty on top; seal the patties at the edges to enclose the cheese. Repeat to form the remaining 3 burgers.
4. Grill the burgers until cooked through, about 5 minutes per side.
5. Spread a Tablespoon of dressing (or homemade ketchup, or both) on the bottom of each toasted bun. Top with the burgers, garnish with the lettuce and tomato, and add the tops of the buns.

for the carrot slaw

In a medium bowl, whisk together the lemon juice, herbes de Provence, honey, grapeseed oil, salt, and pepper. Add the shredded carrots and toss to combine.

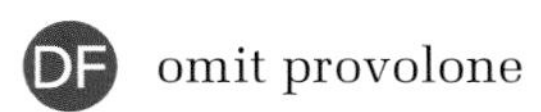

omit provolone

POLENTA PAN PIZZA

I've got a secret weapon for anyone on a restricted gluten-free diet. Cornmeal. Grilled on a baking sheet, this version of pizza is a quick and easy substitute for flour crusts. Polenta is cooked and then spread into a thin layer. Traditional toppings of basil, tomatoes, and fresh mozzarella bring the flavors of summer to the table. Why not create a pizza bar?

Serves 5: 30 minutes  

Olive oil for the pan

3 cups low-sodium chicken or vegetable broth

½ teaspoon kosher salt

¼ teaspoon black pepper

1 teaspoon dried oregano

1 cup quick-cooking polenta or cornmeal, medium grain

1 pound heirloom tomatoes, cored and sliced

2 teaspoons herbes de Provence

6 ounces mozzarella cheese, shredded or cut into thin circles (about 2½ cups)

5 fresh basil leaves, torn

1. Lightly oil a 13-x-18-inch half sheet pan.

2. Bring the broth to boil in a large saucepan. Add the salt, pepper, and oregano, reduce the heat to a simmer, and whisk in the polenta. Cook, stirring constantly, for about 5 minutes, until the polenta starts to thicken.

3. Pour the polenta onto the half sheet pan, spreading it out in an even 1-inch layer. Set aside to cool.

4. Prepare an outdoor grill for indirect grilling.

5. In a medium bowl, combine the tomatoes and herbes de Provence.

6. Sprinkle or scatter the mozzarella over the polenta in an even layer. Top with a layer of the tomatoes and follow with the basil leaves.

7. Set the pan on the cooler part of the grill, close the lid, and grill for 10 minutes, or until the cheese is melted and the edges of the polenta are starting to brown.

Oven alternative

Preheat the oven to 375°F. Place the pan in the oven and bake for 12 minutes, or until the cheese is melted.

Summer Week II:
Thursday

Summer Week II: Friday

SUMMER SMORGASBORD

with Shredded Carrots

Let's face it, sometimes cooking just doesn't seem like fun. There are days we'd all rather be playing kickball in the front yard and eating ice cream. The Scandinavian tradition of the smorgasbord—simple buffet of meats, cheeses, and cold salads—will get you in and out of the kitchen in very little time. After all, you're needed on the front-yard field. It's also an excellent way to clean out the fridge at the end of the week. Visit a trusted neighborhood deli for a choice selection of meats and cheeses.

Serves 4: 15 minutes

for the summer smorgasbord

2 whole wheat pitas, cut in half

Butter lettuce leaves (optional)

2 Tablespoons Dijon mustard

1 red bell pepper, cored, seeded, and thinly sliced

1 yellow or orange bell pepper, cored, seeded, and thinly sliced

1 cucumber, peeled, cut into sticks

4 ounces thinly sliced salami

4 ounces thinly sliced lean turkey breast

4 ounces mozzarella, cut into thin slices

4 slices thinly sliced provolone cheese

6 ounces grape or cherry tomatoes (about 1 cup)

¼ red onion

for the summer smorgasbord

On a large platter or cutting board, arrange the pitas, lettuce, if using, a small bowl of the mustard, and all the remaining ingredients (including the carrots). Let your family assemble their own pitas.

for the shredded carrots

3 medium carrots, peeled and shredded

1 Tablespoon white wine vinegar

1 Tablespoon olive oil

Pinch of kosher salt

Pinch of black pepper

In a small bowl, toss the shredded carrots with the white wine vinegar, olive oil, salt, and pepper.

FAMILY FOOD CULTURE
Gluten Free
the ahern family

SHAUNA: Gluten-Free Girl

DANNY: The Chef

LUCY: Broadway Star in Training

Reported food allergies are increasing every year. Food is such a lifeline to family happiness and learning to deal with allergies can be challenging for many families. But the Ahern kitchen is gluten free and their family food culture is vibrant and fulfilling with a lot of laughter.

Shauna Ahern was diagnosed with celiac disease in the spring of 2005. Overnight she changed her diet, and she has not looked back since. She has become a gluten-free lifestyle expert. There is a misconception that gluten free means giving up good food. For Shauna, it means waking up to food.

The Aherns live and work on Vashon Island, outside of Seattle. Danny is a chef by trade, Shauna is a writer, and the youngest Ahern, Lucy, is the resident Broadway musical enthusiast. *Singin' in the Rain* happens to be a favorite.

The Aherns believe "in order to be well, eat well." This means good-quality, seasonal ingredients, shopping at farmers' markets, and maintaining a first-name basis with the fishmonger and meat purveyor. It is no accident the Aherns settled on Vashon Island. The community is crazy about food quality.

"Being a 'foodie' is the norm here, and caring about food is natural," Shauna says. Vashon neighbors are closely connected to the food chain. One raises chickens, while not far up the road is an organic goat farm. Shauna grew up on the same American "delicacies" enjoyed by most kids in the '70s and '80s, including processed foods. Her family food culture changed when she was diagnosed with celiac disease and eating fresh became necessary for her health and happiness.

Brunch these days might be an asparagus frittata with rhubarb sparkling water and a field greens salad tossed in a light Dijon vinaigrette.

For the Aherns, there is never a rush to leave the table. Life is about enjoying the moments food brings to the family table. Four-year-old Lucy has been known to request salad in lieu of sweets and has not yet cultivated any major food aversions. Eating well-prepared food in season is a big factor.

The entire family works in the garden. Visitors are rewarded with fresh, seasonal meals served over conversations and laughter. Gluten free looks pretty happy.

ahern family food culture

SPECIAL DIET: Gluten free

WHO COOKS: Danny is the main chef, but everyone participates

FAVORITE FAMILY MEAL: Roasted chicken and seasonal vegetables

LEAST FAVORITE MEAL: Junk food

STRICT RULE: Laugh in the kitchen

INDULGENCE: Chocolate chips and ice cream

BEST ADVICE FOR HEALTH: Get rid of the guilt and use moderation

HARDEST TREAT TO GIVE UP: Family time

ON THE NO-EAT LIST: Wheat, rye, barley

SUMMER MENU

MONDAY
Rib-eye and Grilled Chile Rellenos

TUESDAY
Fish Tacos
with Limeade

WEDNESDAY
Balsamic Zucchini-Ricotta Rolls
with Brown Rice and Corn

THURSDAY
Asian Beef Salad

FRIDAY
Roasted-Vegetable Pasta Primavera

SHOPPING LIST

Meat/Seafood

2½ pounds bone-in rib-eye steaks
1¼ pounds skinless fish fillets (any variety), 1 inch thick

Vegetables/Fruit

1 red onion
One 1- to 2-inch piece fresh ginger
1 head Bibb lettuce
8 medium radishes
½ bunch fresh basil
½ bunch fresh mint
½ bunch fresh cilantro
6 medium zucchini
10 ears corn in the husk
1 lemon
11 limes
2 medium tomatoes
4 poblano chiles
1 avocado

Dairy

1 cup ricotta cheese (see DIY ricotta, pages 163–5)
1 cup low-fat plain Greek yogurt
6 slices Monterey Jack cheese

Bakery/Misc.

8 corn tortillas, 6-inch size (see DIY Corn Tortillas, pages 105–6)
Two 15-ounce cans cannellini beans

From the Pantry

2¼ teaspoons kosher salt
2¼ teaspoon black pepper
1 teaspoon sweet Hungarian paprika
½ teaspoon ground cumin
2 Tablespoons rice wine vinegar
5 Tablespoons olive oil
1½ Tablespoons sesame oil
½ cup balsamic vinegar
4 garlic cloves
1 Tablespoon plus ½ cup honey
2½ cups brown rice (dry)
1½ Tablespoons reduced-sodium soy sauce
2 Tablespoons The Fresh 20 Spice Blend (page xxii)
12 ounces whole wheat linguine or spaghetti

PREP AHEAD

Brown Rice for Wednesday and Thursday

Prepare 5 cups brown rice (see page xvii).

Dressing for Thursday

1½ Tablespoons reduced-sodium soy sauce

1½ teaspoons grated fresh ginger

2 garlic cloves, minced or pressed

1½ Tablespoons sesame oil

2 Tablespoons rice wine vinegar

1 Tablespoon honey

Whisk all the ingredients together in a small bowl. Store the dressing in an airtight container in the refrigerator for up to 5 days.

Yield: ⅓ cup

Roasted Poblano Chiles for Monday

4 poblano chiles

1. Preheat an outdoor grill to high.
2. Arrange the poblano chiles over the grill and turn frequently until blackened on all sides.
3. Transfer the chiles to a brown paper lunch bag or large Ziploc bag and let steam for 5 minutes.
4. Remove the skin from the peppers and store whole in their juices for up to 3 days.

Salsa for Tuesday

2 medium tomatoes, chopped

¼ red onion, finely chopped

2 Tablespoons freshly chopped cilantro

Juice of 1 lime

¼ teaspoon kosher salt

¼ teaspoon black pepper

Combine the tomatoes, red onion, cilantro, and lime juice in a bowl. Season with the salt and black pepper. Store in an airtight container in the refrigerator for up to 3 days.

fresh herbs

Nothing improved my cooking more than incorporating fresh herbs. The Fresh 20 recipes use a handful of common herbs that are easy to find: parsley, thyme, and basil. Look for bright, blemish-free leaves. Set the stems in a glass of water and store in the refrigerator, or remove the leaves, wrap in a paper towel, place in a Ziploc bag, and store in the crisper. It is important when storing fresh herbs to keep them dry.

Most commonly used in our recipes

basil
mint
rosemary
cilantro
parsley
thyme
sage
dill

Herb Tips

- Extra herbs can be air-dried for later use in soups or stews.
- Fresh herb leaves can be frozen with a little water in ice trays and then added directly to the pot to unlock the flavor within the cubes.
- In most recipes, fresh herbs are added toward the end of the cooking process.

Summer Week III: Monday

RIB-EYE AND GRILLED CHILE RELLENOS

My husband enjoys a perfectly grilled rib-eye steak more than, well, most things. I stuff roasted poblano chiles with cheese and corn, then grill them next to the steak. It's a decadent meal, but I've been good and so has he, so this is our treat. Don't be afraid of the cost of the rib-eye. It makes two meals this week. There are many other ways to save on the grocery bill this week. Splurge!

Serves 4: 25 minutes

- 2½ pounds bone-in rib-eye steaks
- 2 Tablespoons The Fresh 20 Spice Blend (page xxii)
- 4 Roasted Poblano Chiles (see Prep Ahead, page 100)
- 6 slices Monterey Jack cheese
- 1 teaspoon black pepper
- ½ teaspoon ground cumin
- Grapeseed oil for brushing the grill
- 4 ears corn in the husk

1. Preheat an outdoor grill to high on one side and medium-high on the other.

2. Pat the steaks dry and rub with the spice blend on both sides.

3. Make a lengthwise slit down one side of each chile and remove the seeds. Stuff each pepper with 1½ slices of the cheese, ¼ teaspoon of the black pepper, and ⅛ teaspoon of the ground cumin.

4. Carefully place the poblanos on a small baking sheet and set over the hottest area of the grill.

5. Brush the medium-high side of the grill with the oil. Arrange the steaks and corn on the grill and cook the steaks for 5 to 7 minutes per side, depending on thickness. Close the lid to allow the cheese in the poblanos to melt.

6. Transfer the steaks and corn to a serving platter, cover with foil, and allow the steaks to rest for 5 minutes before serving. Remove the husk from the corn.

Leftover Note: Store ¾ pound of the steak in an airtight container in the refrigerator for dinner on Thursday.

serve the poblanos without cheese

DIY
corn tortillas

There are some excellent commercial tortillas on the market, but they all pale in comparison to freshly made corn tortillas. Homemade tortillas are one of my true pleasures of the kitchen. Minimal ingredients and time partner with a simple technique to create a delicious end product every time. It doesn't get better.

I shape the tortillas by hand, but a tortilla press helps make the job easy; these can be found at Hispanic markets or restaurant supply stores. Purists use only masa harina (corn flour) and water, but I was told adding a pinch of sweet paprika to the dough elevates the flavor just enough to make the tortillas outstanding, and I'd have to agree.

Makes 12 tortillas

- 2 cups masa harina (I use Bob's Red Mill; see Resources, page 263)
- 1 cup warm water
- ½ teaspoon kosher salt
- ¼ teaspoon sweet Hungarian paprika

1. Combine all the ingredients in a deep bowl and mix with your hands until a soft dough forms.

2. Knead the dough a few times on a clean countertop until it forms a smooth ball. Place the dough back in the bowl, cover with plastic wrap, and let rest for 30 minutes.

3. Divide the dough into 12 equal pieces. Roll each piece into a smooth ball by rolling it under the palm of your hand on a floured countertop. Place the balls in a dish and cover with a cloth or plastic wrap so they won't dry out.

4. One at a time, place each dough ball in a gallon-sized Ziploc bag (leave the bag unzipped) and flatten the ball with the palm of your hand. Then, using a rolling pin, roll the dough, still in the bag, into a 5-inch-wide circle. Remove the dough from the bag and transfer it to a covered pot, to prevent it from drying out.

5. Heat a skillet over medium-low heat. Place one tortilla in the pan and cook for about 45 seconds, then turn and cook for another 45 seconds to 1 minute. Transfer the tortilla to a covered pot, this time to keep warm. Repeat with the remaining tortillas.

Tips

- Keep the dough moist.
- Make sure to flatten the tortillas as much as possible. You don't want them too thick.
- Rub the tortillas with a little lime juice.

Add-ins

The combinations are endless for creative tortillas!

- A teaspoon of cinnamon for a sweet version.
- A teaspoon of cayenne pepper to bring on the heat.
- Finely chopped cilantro or parsley to intensify the flavor.
- Grated cheese.
- Grated dark chocolate to balance any spicy fillings.

Serving Ideas

- Add a little grated chocolate to the mix and fill with sautéed bananas.
- Use the finished tortillas to make a batch of chips.

FISH TACOS

with Limeade

In my kitchen, tacos are like pasta. Flexible. This recipe is just one of a hundred different ways you can fix them. Most families enjoy the ease and simplicity of a good taco night. Buy a thick piece of fish and cut it into uniform pieces that will cook evenly, without drying out. You can use the DIY Corn Tortillas on pages 105–6 or store-bought tortillas.

Serves 4: 20 minutes 

for the fish

1¼ pounds skinless fish fillets (any variety), 1 inch thick

¾ teaspoon kosher salt

½ teaspoon black pepper

½ teaspoon sweet paprika

2 Tablespoons olive oil

for the beans

Two 15-ounce cans cannellini beans, rinsed and drained

½ teaspoon sweet paprika

¼ teaspoon kosher salt

for the tacos

8 corn tortillas, 6-inch size

¼ red onion, thinly sliced

5 medium radishes, thinly sliced

½ cup fresh cilantro leaves

1 cup low-fat plain Greek yogurt

2 limes, cut into wedges

1 avocado, sliced

Salsa (see Prep Ahead, page 100)

for the fish

1. Rinse the fish fillets and pat dry. Season with the salt, pepper, and paprika.

2. Heat a large skillet over medium-high heat and add the oil. Once the oil sizzles, add the fish and cook for 2 minutes or so per side, depending on thickness; be careful not to overcook the fish.

for the beans

Meanwhile, combine the beans, paprika, and salt in a medium saucepan and bring to a simmer over medium heat.

for the tacos

1. Wrap the tortillas in a paper towel and heat in the microwave for 20 to 30 seconds.

2. Set out the red onion, radishes, cilantro, yogurt, limes, avocado, beans, and salsa, along with the fish and tortillas, and have each person assemble their own tacos. Serve with the limeade (see opposite).

a fresh idea:

LIMEADE

This summer thirst quencher shows how simple it is to spruce up plain ole water to add dimension to any meal. You can replace the limes with lemons, berries, cucumber, or watermelon. In Mexico, this is called ***agua fresca***, and it keeps everyone well hydrated during those hot summer days.

½ cup honey
½ cup hot water
Juice of 6 limes
Ice cubes

1. In a small bowl, melt the honey in the hot water. Add the lime juice.

2. Fill a 3-quart pitcher with ice. Pour in the honey-lime juice, then fill with cold water. Stir. Serve over ice.

Note: For any agua fresca, *puree the main flavor ingredients with honey and water until well blended. Serve over ice.*

Summer Week III: Wednesday

BALSAMIC ZUCCHINI–RICOTTA ROLLS

with Brown Rice and Corn

This dish is commonly served as an appetizer, but as with so many summer dinners, appetizers work overtime as entrées. Soaking the zucchini in balsamic is what makes this recipe special. The caramelized effect once grilled is simply heavenly. Check out the homemade ricotta recipe on pages 163–5.

Serves 4: 35 minutes  

6 ears corn in the husk

for the balsamic zucchini-ricotta rolls

½ cup balsamic vinegar

6 zucchini, sliced lengthwise into ¼-inch slices (about 5 slices per zucchini)

1 Tablespoon olive oil

½ teaspoon kosher salt

1 cup ricotta cheese

¼ teaspoon black pepper, plus more to taste

Grated zest and juice of 1 lemon

½ cup fresh basil leaves, chopped

2 cups prepared brown rice, reheated

1. Preheat an outdoor grill to high on one side.
2. Set the corn on the cooler part of the grill for 10 minutes.
3. Remove the corn from the grill and allow to cool, then remove the husk silk before serving.

Leftover Note: Store 2 ears of the corn in an airtight container in the refrigerator for dinner on Friday night.

for the balsamic zucchini-ricotta rolls

1. Toss the zucchini in the balsamic vinegar and let stand for 5 to 10 minutes.
2. Lightly brush the zucchini pieces on both sides with the oil. Season with the salt. Arrange the zucchini on the grill in one layer and cook for 3 minutes per side, or until it is soft with golden-brown grill marks. Remove the zucchini from the grill and allow to cool.
3. Meanwhile, in a small bowl, mix the ricotta cheese with the pepper, 1 teaspoon of the lemon zest, the lemon juice, and the basil.
4. Spread a layer of the ricotta mix over one side of each zucchini slice. Roll up each slice from one end to the other and press to seal.

Leftover Note: Store 8 slices of the zucchini and ½ cup of the ricotta blend in airtight containers in the refrigerator for dinner on Friday.

5. Serve the zucchini rolls over the brown rice, with the corn.

ASIAN BEEF SALAD

This salad works well with any leftover beef, but rib-eye elevates the dish. Purists will notice that I replace the traditional fish sauce with rice wine vinegar and honey. For me, the mint and chiles are the real flavor builders.

Serves 4: 15 minutes  

¾ pound leftover rib-eye steak (see Monday, page 103), sliced

Dressing (see Prep Ahead, page 100)

1 head Bibb lettuce, separated into leaves, washed, dried, and shredded (4 cups)

3 cups prepared brown rice

3 radishes, thinly sliced

4 fresh basil leaves, shredded

2 limes, cut into wedges

¼ cup fresh mint leaves

1. Marinate the steak slices in half of the dressing for 10 minutes.

2. Toss the lettuce and brown rice with the other half of the dressing.

3. Divide the lettuce and rice among serving bowls. Top with the steak, radishes, and basil. Garnish with the lime wedges and mint.

Summer Week III: Thursday

Summer Week III: Friday

ROASTED-VEGETABLE PASTA PRIMAVERA

The one thing I can say about summer pasta is that it belongs with grilled vegetables. This recipe has most likely been served by nonnas up and down the coasts of Italy for generations. Freshly ground black pepper and creamy ricotta send this basic recipe into the stratosphere of delicious. It's a lot of bang for your summer buck in fewer than 20 minutes.

Serves 4: 20 minutes 

12 ounces whole wheat linguine or spaghetti

2 Tablespoons olive oil

½ red onion, chopped

2 garlic cloves, minced

8 leftover grilled zucchini slices (see Wednesday, page 111), chopped

2 ears leftover grilled corn (see Wednesday, page 111), kernels removed

½ teaspoon kosher salt

¼ teaspoon black pepper

½ cup leftover ricotta cheese mix (see Wednesday, page 111)

1. Bring a large pot of salted water to a boil. Add the pasta and cook until al dente, about 9 minutes. Drain the pasta, reserving ½ cup of the pasta water, and return it to the pot.

2. Meanwhile, heat the olive oil in a large skillet over medium-high heat. Add the red onion and garlic and sauté until soft, about 4 minutes. Mix in the zucchini and corn and heat through.

3. Toss the pasta with the vegetables. If dry, add a Tablespoon of reserved pasta water at a time until it reaches the desired creaminess. Season with the salt and pepper. Top each serving with a dollop of the ricotta cheese blend.

DIY *salsa*

Salsa is a food group in my kitchen and I use it for everything from an after-school snack to an omelet topper.

Salsa comes in many varieties. Chiles, tomatoes, lime, and salt in the form of pico de gallo is the original Mexican salsa, but salsa has the ability to assume the cultural undertones of many nations. Italian tomatoes, garlic, and olive oil is a salsa; Caribbean fruit with lime and onion is another version. Experiment with these combinations or invent your own!

Yield: 2 cups

- 2 medium tomatoes, chopped
- Juice of 1 lime
- ¼ onion, chopped
- 2 garlic cloves, minced or pressed
- 2 Tablespoons chopped fresh cilantro
- ½ teaspoon kosher salt
- ¼ teaspoon black pepper
- ½ jalapeño pepper, finely chopped (optional)

1. Combine all the ingredients in a medium bowl.
2. Cover and let sit at room temperature for at least 20 minutes. The salsa can be stored in an airtight container in the refrigerator for up to 2 days.

SUMMER MENU

MONDAY

Honey Lime Drumsticks
with Watermelon Salad

TUESDAY

Avocado Pesto Pasta

WEDNESDAY

Chile Pork Kebabs
with Pesto Corn and Watermelon

THURSDAY

Chef Louise's Crab and Corn Chowder
with Tomato Quinoa Salad

FRIDAY

Caribbean Pork Salad

SHOPPING LIST

Meat/Seafood

8 ounces lump crab meat
1½ pounds pork tenderloin
8 chicken drumsticks (about 1½ pounds)

Vegetables/Fruits

10 ears corn in the husk
3 avocados
4 medium tomatoes
¾ red onion
1 head red leaf lettuce
⅓ cup plus 2 Tablespoons fresh mint leaves
1 large bunch fresh basil
½ bunch fresh cilantro
1 small watermelon
1½ lemons
3 limes
2 ripe mangoes
1 serrano pepper

Dairy

⅓ cup feta cheese, crumbled
1 cup grated Parmesan cheese

Bakery/Misc.

One 15-ounce can black beans
1 cup walnuts
¼ cup pine nuts (optional; see Caribbean Pork Salad, page 131)
2 cups quinoa (dry)

From the Pantry

3 teaspoons kosher salt
1½ teaspoons black pepper
1¼ teaspoons sweet Hungarian paprika
1⅛ teaspoons cayenne pepper
1 Tablespoon chili powder
3 teaspoons ground cumin
¾ cup olive oil
¼ cup grapeseed oil
¼ cup rice wine vinegar
8 garlic cloves
5 Tablespoons honey
¼ cup Pantry Dressing of your choice
12 ounces whole wheat spaghetti
3 cups low-sodium chicken or vegetable broth

PREP AHEAD

Marinated Chicken for Monday

- Grated zest and juice of 2 limes
- 3 Tablespoons honey
- 3 Tablespoons grapeseed oil
- 2 garlic cloves, minced or pressed
- 8 chicken drumsticks (about 1½ pounds)
- ½ teaspoon kosher salt
- ¼ teaspoon black pepper
- ¼ teaspoon sweet Hungarian paprika

1. Whisk together the lime zest and juice, honey, oil, and garlic in a small bowl.

2. Season the drumsticks with the salt, pepper, and paprika and arrange in a glass container.

3. Pour the marinade over the drumsticks, seal the container, and marinate in the refrigerator for at least 2 hours, and up to 24 hours.

Pesto for Tuesday and Wednesday

- 1 cup walnuts, toasted
- 4 garlic cloves
- Grated zest of 1 lemon
- 2 Tablespoons fresh lemon juice
- ⅛ teaspoon cayenne pepper
- 2 cups packed fresh basil leaves
- 1 cup grated Parmesan cheese
- 1 teaspoon kosher salt
- ½ teaspoon black pepper
- ½ cup olive oil, plus more if needed

1. In the bowl of a food processor, combine the walnuts, garlic, lemon zest, lemon juice, cayenne pepper, basil, cheese, salt, and pepper and pulse until well blended.

2. With the food processor running, stream in the olive oil until smooth, about 1 minute. If the pesto is too thick, add more olive oil or some water.

3. Transfer the pesto to an airtight container and place a layer of plastic wrap on top of the pesto to help prevent browning. Seal the container and store in the refrigerator for up to a week.

Quinoa for Thursday and Friday

Prepare 4 cups quinoa (see page xvii).

Dressing for Friday

- 3 Tablespoons olive oil
- ¼ cup rice wine vinegar
- 2 Tablespoons honey
- 2 Tablespoons chopped fresh mint
- ¼ teaspoon kosher salt
- ¼ teaspoon black pepper

Whisk together all the ingredients in a small bowl until smooth and creamy. Store the dressing in an airtight container in the refrigerator for up to 5 days.

junk food wars

Yes, sometimes I am THAT mom and I ask my boys to politely decline the soccer snack doughnuts after a ninety-minute game in the hot sun. I am not riding on my high horse. Weekends are a constant battle for balance, and as the mother of two active boys, I monitor and support the fuel and energy needed for them to complete a long day of sports. There is quite often a hot dog discussion. For me, the answer to hot dogs is always no, but I'll admit I'm not always right. Moderation is an important part of any family food culture, and although we do not serve hot dogs at our house, the kids may indulge at other venues on special occasions. Here are three easy steps to battling junk food.

1. Do not keep junk food in the house. Anywhere. If there is a bag of potato chips, you will surely eat it.
2. Keep healthy snacks in your bag and in the car for when the kids suddenly get hungry.
3. Negotiate specific treat times, like one day a week for cookies or one Sunday a month as doughnut day. This gives everyone something fun to look forward to.

Summer Week IV:
Monday

HONEY LIME DRUMSTICKS

with Watermelon Salad

In our house, we call these margarita legs because of their salty-sweet flavor. Easy to prepare, they are quintessentially summer. If you grill them on the weekend, they make a fast, kid-approved dinner during the week. Serve hot or cold.

Serves 4: 20 minutes 

Marinated Chicken (see Prep Ahead, page 120)

for the watermelon salad

½ small watermelon, cut into cubes

⅓ cup fresh mint leaves, chopped

⅓ cup feta cheese, crumbled

1. Preheat an outdoor grill.
2. Remove the drumsticks from the marinade (discard the marinade), arrange the drumsticks on the grill over a medium flame, and cook for 15 minutes, rotating the drumsticks every 3 minutes or so, until 165°F and juices run clear.

for the watermelon salad

In a large bowl, toss the watermelon cubes with the mint and feta. Serve with the chicken.

 omit feta

AVOCADO PESTO PASTA

Pesto and avocado are two of my favorite things, so this pasta is the best of both worlds. The avocado gives the pesto a creamy texture. Save a little to use as vegetable dip or to garnish breakfast eggs. I sometimes slather this pesto over sliced fresh tomatoes and call it lunch.

Serves 4–5: 15 minutes 

12 ounces whole wheat spaghetti

1 cup Pesto (see Prep Ahead, page 120)

2 avocados, halved and pitted

Juice of ½ lemon

2 medium tomatoes, sliced

1. Bring a large pot of salted water to a boil. Add the pasta and cook until al dente. Drain, reserving ½ cup of the cooking liquid.

2. Put the pesto in a large bowl. Scoop the avocado flesh into the bowl and mash the avocado and lemon juice into the pesto.

3. Toss the pasta with the pesto, adding some of the reserved pasta water if necessary to give it the desired consistency.

4. Serve the pasta with the sliced tomatoes.

Summer Week IV: Tuesday

Summer Week IV:
Wednesday

CHILE PORK KEBABS

with Pesto Corn and Watermelon

The ease of kebabs on the grill is one of summer's delights. Another is basil and corn. With this meal you get all three. This pesto can be used as a bread spread, egg topper, or pizza topping, but on grilled corn, it is finger-lickin' good.

Serves 4: 25 minutes 

for the chile pork kebabs

2 teaspoons ground cumin

1 teaspoon cayenne pepper

½ teaspoon kosher salt

½ teaspoon black pepper

1½ pounds pork tenderloin, cut into 2-inch cubes

4 to 8 skewers (if wooden, soak in water for 10 minutes)

1 Tablespoon grapeseed oil

for the pesto corn

6 ears corn in the husk

½ cup Pesto (see Prep Ahead, page 120)

½ small watermelon, cut into wedges

for the chile pork kebabs

1. Preheat an outdoor grill.
2. Combine the spices in a medium bowl. Toss with the pork to coat, rubbing the seasonings into the pork with your hands. Place 4 or more pork cubes on each skewer.
3. Brush the grill with the oil. Arrange the pork skewers over direct heat on the grill and the corn (in the husks) over indirect heat. Put the lid on the grill. Cook the pork, turning the skewers often, until browned on all sides, 6 to 8 minutes total. Cook the corn, turning it once or twice, for 10 to 15 minutes. Let cool before serving.

Leftover Note: Store 2 cups of the cubed pork in an airtight container in the refrigerator for dinner on Friday.

for the pesto corn

1. Spread the pesto on the corn, and serve with the pork and watermelon wedges.

 omit pesto

LOUISE'S CRAB AND CORN CHOWDER

with Tomato Quinoa Salad

Chef Louise Mellor gets high marks for this soup-and-salad combo. Subscribers ranked this dish as one of the top summer meals. A little crab goes a long way in this recipe. Quality canned crab from a fishmonger is perfectly fine to use if fresh is not available.

Serves 4: 30 minutes  

for the crab and corn chowder

1 Tablespoon olive oil

½ medium red onion, finely chopped

2 garlic cloves, minced or pressed

¼ serrano pepper, minced (about 1 teaspoon)

4 ears corn, husked and kernels removed, cobs reserved

1 Tablespoon chili powder

1 teaspoon ground cumin

1 teaspoon sweet Hungarian paprika

3 cups low-sodium chicken or vegetable broth

1 cup water

½ bunch fresh cilantro leaves, roughly chopped

8 ounces lump crabmeat, picked over to remove any cartilage

Juice of 1 lime

¾ teaspoon kosher salt

for the crab and corn chowder

1. Heat a large pot over medium heat. Add the oil, and once it is hot, add the onion, garlic, serrano pepper, and corn. Stir to combine and cook for 2 to 3 minutes, until the onions become soft and translucent.

2. Add the chili powder, cumin, and paprika and stir to combine. Turn up the heat to medium-high and add the chicken broth and water, stirring to combine. Add the reserved corncobs, bring to a simmer, and simmer for 12 to 15 minutes.

3. Remove the corncobs. Carefully ladle 2 cups of the chowder, with vegetables, into a blender and blend until smooth (be sure to hold the lid of the blender down with a towel tightly; hot liquid will create steam pressure in the blender).

4. Add the pureed chowder back to the pot and stir to combine. Reduce the heat to low and add the cilantro, crabmeat, lime juice, and salt. Stir gently and cook for 5 minutes.

5. Taste and adjust the seasoning; adjust the thickness by adding more water if needed.

for the tomato quinoa salad

- 2 cups prepared quinoa, at room temperature (see page xvii)
- 2 tomatoes, cut into wedges
- 1 avocado, halved, pitted, peeled, and cut into cubes
- ¼ cup Pantry Dressing of your choice (pages 26–7)

for the tomato quinoa salad

Combine the quinoa with the tomatoes and avocado in a bowl. Toss with the dressing.

Summer Week IV: Thursday

beyond iceberg

Whether giving crunch to a burger or sandwich or taking the spotlight in a salad, lettuce is an integral part of the family kitchen. The Fresh 20 uses a few common salad varieties to complete everyday meals, but I encourage you to experiment with a new leaf once in a while and make substitutions whenever you can.

My top picks:

- Romaine
- Arugula
- Butter Leaf, such as Bibb
- Red Leaf
- Endive
- Radicchio
- Spinach

Keeping Greens Fresh

As soon as you get salad greens home, wash and dry them, wrap in paper towels, and store in a Ziploc bag in the crisper. When properly prepped, they will keep for up to a week. If you have a salad spinner, let kids enjoy the task of drying the greens.

CARIBBEAN PORK SALAD

Summer salads are the best part of the warm-weather months. Well, ice cream ranks high—but only after a delicious salad. Mixing some West Indies flavors into this salad just feels right. There are several YouTube videos showcasing mango peeling and pitting.

1 head (8 cups) red leaf lettuce, torn into small pieces

2 cups prepared quinoa (see page xvii)

Dressing (see Prep Ahead, page 121)

2 ripe mangoes, peeled, pitted, and cubed

¼ small red onion, thinly sliced

One 15-ounce can black beans, drained and rinsed

4 to 5 fresh basil leaves, slivered

2 cups leftover pork tenderloin (see Wednesday, page 127)

¼ cup pine nuts (optional)

1. In a large salad bowl, toss the lettuce and quinoa with the dressing. Fold in the mangoes, red onion, beans, and basil. Top with the pieces of pork.

2. If desired, sprinkle the salad with the pine nuts.

Summer Week IV: Friday

FAMILY FOOD CULTURE
Unprocessed

the sellers family

LISA, holistic health practitioner, short-order breakfast cook, management consultant

DUSTIN, CEO, sportsman, and boat captain; likes peanut butter—a lot

MAXXWELL, teenager, skateboarder, eats everything, says thank you

PARIS, allergic to gluten, soy, eggs, and cow's milk; packs lunch and soccer snacks

QUINN, Hawaiian forager

In my early twenties, a dear friend's parents opened to me a whole new world of fresh food. The preparations for dinner at Tom and Sherri Sellers' home started early in the day with soaking beans and preparing masa for homemade tortillas. Fresh herbs picked from their vast garden enhanced homemade stocks. The family relied on the best-quality meats, purchased in small luxurious packages, to add maximum flavor to their dishes.

It was not about the abundance of the food, it was about the quality. Nothing at the Sellers' house was packaged. No sauce from a jar, no frozen ingredients. It was 1992 and the copies of *Bon Appétit* and *Gourmet* I found scattered around their home were dog-eared and worn from constant use. Eating fresh seasonal ingredients was their family food culture and dinners were where they showcased the fruits of their labors.

Luckily for me, my dearest friend, Lisa, married the Sellers' son Dustin, and we have shared many meals around Tom and Sherri's table. And today with three children, Lisa and Dustin continue the family food culture in their own kitchen. Lisa became the first The Fresh 20 client back in 2008 when she offered me her firstborn in exchange for a dinner plan. She was out of ideas and short on time, and she needed a little help from a friend who knew her way around the kitchen.

Lisa and Dustin's family is the busiest one I know. Sports, music, and art keep their schedule full until dinnertime, but The Fresh 20 has allowed them to continue their family food culture by planning ahead for weeknight dinners. Continuing the idea of freshness learned from her in-laws, Lisa has always kept a small herb garden and cooked using the very best seasonal ingredients.

sellers family food culture

SPECIAL OR RESTRICTED DIET: Multidiet household; dairy free, egg free, gluten free

WHO COOKS MOST MEALS?: Lisa

FAVORITE FAMILY MEAL: Rice bowl

LEAST FAVORITE MEAL: Overcooked fish

STRICT RULE: Eat together

INDULGENCE: Restaurant desserts

BEST ADVICE FOR HEALTH: Drink water

HARDEST TREAT TO GIVE UP: Coffee

ON THE NO-EAT LIST: Nacho cheese spread

IN SEASON
Apples
Broccoli
Brussels sprouts
Carrots
Cauliflower
Celery
Cranberries
Eggplant
Fennel
Garlic
Mushrooms
Nuts
Onions
Parsley
Pears
Potatoes
Pumpkin
Sage
Spinach
Thyme

FALL

I'm always ready for fall. After summer fun, I appreciate the quiet house and some uninterrupted time when the kids return to school. When people talk about spring cleaning, I always feel out of step. Fall is the time I reorganize, clean cupboards, recommit to my meal plans, and get a little more structured and formal with dinner schedules and homework. There are two times a year when people are most apt to change their eating habits, January and September. The New Year's resolution has never worked for me. But fall has that back-to-school enthusiasm: I feel like I can do just about anything. This is the perfect time for you to restock your pantry and recommit to healthy, homemade dinners.

The weekends seem busier in the fall, so I am more likely to cook ahead and freeze things, especially soups and stews and casseroles. I want to enjoy every second of that last golden light of an October evening with my family and not worry about getting home before the sun dips in order to get dinner on the table.

It's comforting how the family begins to drift from the backyard into the kitchen in the fall. We start to stay at the table longer. It might be homework avoidance; it also might be that the family recipes I inherited play a larger role on the table. My mother's chicken and dumplings, my dad's spaghetti and meatballs, Auntie Neats's gumbo (well, my version; she hasn't given hers up yet). The late fall holidays—Thanksgiving in particular—take us back to old-fashioned family gatherings. Call me nostalgic.

My own kitchen habits head back to one-pot dishes and casseroles—*casserole*, by the way, is not a four-letter word. Every great culinary tradition has its casseroles. Consider the French cassoulet, the Spanish paella, the Italian lasagna. But fresh ingredients make the difference between good casseroles and goop. I love to make homemade ricotta to help lighten my fall casseroles. I include that recipe in this chapter, although a high-quality commercial ricotta works just fine.

The first of the season's winter squash, garlic-festival garlic, apples, pears, and warming broth—yes, autumn is as much about these foods as it is about back to school, sports games, and starting to warm up the kitchen again.

FALL MENU

MONDAY

Mimi's Chicken and Dumplings

TUESDAY

Buttery Broiled Fish 'n' Leeks with Carrots

WEDNESDAY

Mushroom Soup with Garlic Toasts and Shaved Fennel Salad

THURSDAY

Chicken Fricassee

FRIDAY

Lemon Fennel Risotto

SHOPPING LIST

Meat/Seafood

One 3½-pound chicken plus 1 pound boneless, skinless chicken thighs

Four 1-inch-thick white fish fillets (about 1½ pounds)

Vegetables/Fruit

4 celery stalks

8 carrots

1 medium onion

¼ bunch chopped fresh flat-leaf parsley

3 Tablespoons fresh thyme leaves

6 medium shallots

4 medium leeks

3 lemons

½ ounce dried porcini mushrooms

3 pounds white button mushrooms

2 small fennel bulbs

Dairy

1 large egg

4 Tablespoons unsalted butter

1 cup plus 2 Tablespoons heavy cream

1 cup grated Parmesan cheese

Bakery/Misc.

1 whole wheat baguette

1¾ cups white wine (such as pinot grigio or sauvignon blanc)

2 cups Arborio rice

From the Pantry

1 cup olive oil

4½ teaspoons kosher salt

2½ teaspoons black pepper

2 teaspoons white wine vinegar

⅛ teaspoon cayenne pepper

2¼ teaspoons ground cumin

1 teaspoon baking powder

13 to 14 cups low-sodium chicken or vegetable broth

11 garlic cloves

1½ cups plus 1 Tablespoon whole wheat flour

PREP AHEAD

Dumplings for Monday

1½ cups whole wheat flour

1 teaspoon baking powder

1 teaspoon kosher salt

1 large egg

½ cup heavy cream

1 Tablespoon olive oil

1 Tablespoon finely chopped fresh flat-leaf parsley

¼ cup water, if needed

1. In a medium bowl, using a fork, combine all the ingredients except the water and mix until a soft dough forms; do not overmix. Add in water if dough becomes too thick.

2. Divide the dough into 12 Tablespoon-sized pieces.

3. Place in a Pyrex dish covered with a wet paper towel and plastic wrap.

mirepoix

I like trios. When I teach cooking, I always start with what many refer to as the holy trinity, mirepoix. A simple mix of onions, celery, and carrots creates a solid base for hundreds of recipes. The term is best known in French cooking circles, but nearly every restaurant uses the combination for stocks and sauces. It's easy to create rich flavors when starting with this trio.

Mirepoix ranges from rustic to refined, depending on the dish. I like to use bite-sized or smaller pieces in most recipes, but for stock, a rough chop works well.

Basic Mirepoix

3 medium carrots

3 celery stalks

1 Tablespoon olive oil

1 medium onion (yellow or white), chopped

1. Peel the carrots and slice them into disks. Cut the disks into quarters. Trim the celery. Cut each stalk lengthwise in half, then chop.
2. Heat the olive oil in a 5-quart Dutch oven or sauté pan over medium-high heat. Add the carrots, celery, and onion and sauté for 5 to 10 minutes, stirring frequently, until the onions are translucent and the carrots have softened. If desired, you can place a sheet of foil or parchment loosely over the pot to let the mirepoix "sweat."
3. Now it's time to add your favorite herbs, followed by a bit of stock. Then you're all set to add chicken, beef, or fish, cover, and cook!

If you learn some very basic cooking trios, you can identify and prepare food from any culture. This has helped me create rich flavors using very few ingredients.

CREOLE/CAJUN:
celery, bell peppers, onion

FRENCH:
onion, celery, carrots (mirepoix)

GREEK:
lemon juice, olive oil, oregano

CHINESE:
scallions, ginger, garlic

INDIAN:
garlic, ginger, onion

INDONESIAN:
coconut, chile peppers, curry

SOUTHERN ITALY:
tomato, garlic, basil

CUBAN:
garlic, bell peppers, onion

SPANISH:
garlic, onion, tomato

WEST AFRICAN:
chile powder, onion, tomato

BE ADVENTUROUS!

Fall Week 1: Monday

MIMI'S CHICKEN AND DUMPLINGS

My mother's signature dish always makes me feel like I'm home again. Incredibly easy to prepare, dumplings are a fun alternative to noodles. I add fresh herbs to Mom's version and prefer a clear broth instead of her thicker sauce.

Serves 4: 40 minutes 

- 2 Tablespoons olive oil
- One 3½-pound chicken, cut into pieces, plus 1 pound boneless, skinless chicken thighs
- 2 celery stalks, coarsely chopped
- 4 carrots, peeled and sliced
- 1 medium onion, chopped
- 2 teaspoons kosher salt
- 1 teaspoon black pepper
- 2 teaspoons ground cumin
- 4 cups low-sodium chicken broth
- 1 cup water, if needed
- 2 Tablespoons chopped fresh flat-leaf parsley

Dumplings (see Prep Ahead, page 138)

1. Heat the olive oil in a large pot over medium-high heat. Add the chicken, and sear on all sides until golden brown, about 10 minutes. Once cooked through, remove the chicken and set aside.

Leftover Note: Store chicken thighs in an airtight container in the refrigerator for dinner on Thursday.

2. Add the celery, carrots, and onion to the same pot and cook for 5 minutes, or until they soften. Stir, scraping the yummy brown bits off the bottom of the pot. Add the salt, pepper, and cumin, stir to combine, and cook for 2 minutes.
3. Add the chicken to the pot and pour in the broth. If there is not enough broth to cover the chicken, add the water. Increase the heat to high and bring the liquid to a boil. Reduce the heat to low, cover the pot, and let the soup simmer for 10 minutes, or until the chicken is no longer pink inside. Sprinkle in the parsley.
4. Carefully drop the dumplings into the simmering broth. When the dumplings rise to the top, cover and simmer the soup for 15 minutes.
5. Divide the chicken and dumplings among bowls and serve immediately.

Note: You can leave the chicken in whole pieces or remove the meat from the bones and return it to the pot for easy serving.

BUTTERY BROILED FISH 'N' LEEKS

with Carrots

I know fish is a hard sell at some family dinner tables, but this dish, which results in buttery and flaky fish, shows how easy and delicious it can be.

Serves 4: 25 minutes 

for the carrots

4 medium carrots, peeled and cut into ½-inch slices

2 Tablespoons fresh thyme leaves, finely chopped

¼ teaspoon ground cumin

⅛ teaspoon cayenne pepper

½ teaspoon black pepper

for the fish

2 Tablespoons unsalted butter

2 Tablespoons olive oil

2 medium shallots, chopped

2 garlic cloves, minced or pressed

2 medium leeks, trimmed and chopped

Grated zest and juice of 1 lemon

Four 1-inch-thick white fish fillets (about 1½ pounds)

½ teaspoon kosher salt

for the carrots

1. Bring a medium pot of water to a boil. Drop the carrots into the boiling water and cook for 5 minutes, or until they are fork-tender but not mushy. Drain the carrots and place them in a medium bowl.
2. Toss the carrots with the thyme, cumin, cayenne, and ¼ teaspoon of the pepper.

for the fish

1. Place a rack 4 inches from the heat and preheat the broiler.
2. Melt the butter with the oil in a small pot over medium heat. Add the shallots and garlic and cook for 1 minute, or until fragrant. Stir in the leeks, lemon zest, and lemon juice and cook until the leeks are softened, about 3 minutes. Remove from the heat.
3. Season the fillets with the salt and the remaining ¼ teaspoon pepper and arrange on a baking sheet. Spoon the leek mixture over the fish and broil for 12 minutes, or until the fish is opaque through the middle and can be easily flaked with a fork.

Fall Week I: Tuesday

MUSHROOM SOUP

with Garlic Toasts and Shaved Fennel Salad

When I was a child, mushrooms and I were not friendly. Thankfully, I outgrew my aversion and now appreciate their rich and earthy flavor. For a very simple, lighter version of this soup, leave out the cream and skip the puree step. Fragrant fennel makes a crisp and easy side.

Serves 4: 30 minutes 

for the mushroom soup

½ ounce dried porcini mushrooms, rinsed well

4 cups hot water

2 Tablespoons unsalted butter

2 Tablespoons olive oil

4 medium shallots, minced

2 garlic cloves, minced or pressed

¼ cup white wine

½ teaspoon kosher salt

½ teaspoon black pepper

2 pounds white button mushrooms, wiped clean and sliced

4 cups low-sodium chicken or vegetable broth

½ cup heavy cream

Juice of 1 lemon

for the garlic toasts

½ whole wheat baguette, cut into ½-inch slices

2 Tablespoons olive oil

3 garlic cloves

for the mushroom soup

1. Soak the dried mushrooms in the hot water for 10 minutes. Drain the mushrooms, reserving ½ cup of the soaking liquid, and set aside.

2. Meanwhile, heat the butter and oil in a Dutch oven or other heavy pot over medium heat. Add the shallots and garlic and sauté for 2 to 3 minutes. Pour in the wine, season with the salt and pepper, and stir to combine.

3. Add the porcini and button mushrooms and cook until the mushrooms begin to soften slightly, about 3 minutes. Add the broth and bring to a boil. Remove from the heat.

4. Transfer the soup in batches to a food processor or blender and puree.

5. Return the pureed soup to the pot and reduce the heat to low. Pour in the cream and lemon juice, bring to a simmer, and simmer the soup for 5 minutes.

Note: Do not fill the processor or blender to the top with hot liquid to avoid a messy explosion!

for the garlic toasts

1. Place a rack 6 inches from the heat and preheat the broiler.

2. Brush the bread with the olive oil and place on a baking sheet. Broil the bread for 1 to 2 minutes, or until it is lightly toasted. Rub the crostini with the garlic and serve with the soup.

for the shaved fennel salad

- 1 small fennel bulb, trimmed and thinly shaved on a mandoline or other vegetable slicer
- 2 Tablespoons roughly chopped fresh flat-leaf parsley
- 2 teaspoons white wine vinegar
- 1 Tablespoon olive oil
- Kosher salt and black pepper to taste

for the shaved fennel salad

In a small bowl, combine the fennel and parsley. Toss with the vinegar, olive oil, and salt and pepper to taste.

Fall Week I: Wednesday

Fall Week I:
Thursday

CHICKEN FRICASSEE

Rural French cooking has produced some of the best dishes I've ever tasted. It's comfort food at the core. You could use leftover chicken for a quick rendition that delivers the same flavor profile in half the time.

Serves 4: 20 minutes

- 2 Tablespoons olive oil
- 2 medium leeks, trimmed and chopped
- 2 celery stalks, finely chopped
- 1 Tablespoon whole wheat flour
- 2 garlic cloves, minced or pressed
- 1 Tablespoon fresh thyme leaves
- 2 cups low-sodium chicken broth
- 1 cup white wine
- 1 pound leftover skinless, boneless chicken thighs (see Monday, page 141)
- 8 ounces white button mushrooms, wiped clean and cut in half
- 2 Tablespoons heavy cream (optional)

- ½ whole wheat baguette, cut into slices and toasted

1. Heat the olive oil in a Dutch oven or other heavy pot over medium heat. Add the leeks and celery and cook until soft, about 5 minutes.
2. Stir in the flour, garlic, and thyme. Cook for 1 to 2 minutes, until the scent of the flour is gone. Pour in the broth and wine and bring to a boil, stirring occasionally. Reduce the heat, add the chicken and mushrooms, and simmer for 5 minutes.
3. Remove from the heat and stir in the cream.
4. Serve the fricassee with the toasted bread for soaking up the sauce.

GF thicken with 2 teaspoons rice flour to replace flour and omit the baguette

DF omit heavy cream

LEMON FENNEL RISOTTO

This is a hands-on dish that never disappoints. It would be wise to recruit someone in the family to help you stir the risotto. Feel free to rename this dish "licorice risotto"—the finely chopped fennel gives it a similar flavor profile—to pique the interest of pickier eaters.

Serves 4: 35 minutes  

2 Tablespoons olive oil

1 small fennel bulb, trimmed and finely chopped

2 garlic cloves, minced or pressed

2 cups Arborio rice

½ teaspoon kosher salt

½ teaspoon black pepper

½ cup white wine (such as pinot grigio or sauvignon blanc)

3 to 4 cups low-sodium chicken or vegetable broth

8 ounces white button mushrooms, wiped clean and sliced

Grated zest of 1 lemon plus 1 Tablespoon fresh lemon juice

1 cup grated Parmesan cheese

1. Heat the oil in a Dutch oven or other heavy pot over medium-high heat. Add the fennel and cook for 3 to 4 minutes, stirring occasionally, until softened and translucent. Stir in the garlic and cook for 1 minute.

2. Add the rice and cook, stirring, until the grains become glossy, about 2 minutes. Season with the salt and pepper. Stir in the wine and cook until it has evaporated, about 5 minutes.

3. Add 2 cups of the broth to the rice mixture and stir to combine. Cook, stirring every 2 to 3 minutes to prevent the rice from sticking to the bottom of the pan, until all the liquid has been absorbed. Add just enough of the broth to cover the rice and continue to cook, stirring. The risotto will begin to become creamier as the grains soften with each addition of broth.

4. Repeat with the remaining broth, then add the mushrooms, lemon zest, and lemon juice. Taste the rice for texture. The risotto should be tender but with a slight firmness, not mushy.

5. Stir in the Parmesan cheese and transfer to bowls for serving.

Fall Week 1: Friday

FAMILY FOOD CULTURE
Working Mom
pam anderson

Raising two children in a healthy household with two working parents in the era of microwaves was no easy task. Pam Anderson kept on cooking. She admits it was not always easy, and there was the occasional takeout fix or restaurant trip, but dinnertime was always family time.

A career in cooking as an editor and author has kept her close to the food world, but nothing compares to the connections made at the dinner table. Her two daughters, Maggy and Sharon, share her love of the kitchen. The family re-creates the passion on Three Many Cooks, a food-related blog about good meals and community.

Pam knows what a task getting everyone to the table can be for a multi-passionate family. When the kids were growing up, meals were a constant priority. She believes breaking bread together fuels confidence in young children.

Her youngest daughter, Maggy, is drawn to how powerful food can be for vitality. Her experience preparing meals with her sister and mother gave her the solid foundation to instill a healthy family food culture in her own life. For Maggy, everything about food became clear when she started to reduce her meat intake and began to listen to her body's reactions to food. Maggy says, "I never knew I was supposed to feel this way." Clean eating has become easy and now her body craves whole foods. She attributes her food confidence to Pam and the consistency of eating together in the midst of being a busy family.

FALL MENU

MONDAY

Aunt Judy's Brisket
with Roasted Potatoes

TUESDAY

Ratatouille Halibut
with Basil Couscous

WEDNESDAY

Braised-Beef Skillet Lasagna
with Green Salad

THURSDAY

Split Pea and Ham Soup
with Crunchy Fall Salad

FRIDAY

Eggplant Caponata Penne

SHOPPING LIST

Meat/Seafood

4 pounds beef brisket
1¼ pounds halibut fillets (or any thick white-fleshed fish)
1 pound lean ham (about a 1-inch-thick slice from the deli)

Vegetables/Fruit

4 medium yellow onions
2 pounds new potatoes
1 zucchini
1 pound eggplant, plus 1 eggplant
3 red bell peppers
½ lemon
2 heads red leaf lettuce
3 medium carrots
2 celery stalks
¼ bunch fresh thyme leaves
½ bunch fresh basil

Dairy

1½ cups part-skim ricotta cheese (see DIY Ricotta, pages 163–5)
1 cup shredded mozzarella cheese

Bakery/Misc.

2 cups dried split peas
Two 15-ounce cans diced tomatoes
⅓ cup hazelnuts
1 cup whole wheat couscous

From the Pantry

3 Tablespoons grapeseed oil
½ cup plus 2 Tablespoons olive oil
2 Tablespoons balsamic vinegar
4 teaspoons kosher salt
2¼ teaspoons black pepper
¼ teaspoon sweet Hungarian paprika
2 Tablespoons plus 2 teaspoons dried oregano
⅓ cup plus 2 Tablespoons tomato paste
11 garlic cloves
5 cups low-sodium chicken or vegetable broth
8 ounces whole wheat penne
8 ounces whole wheat lasagna noodles
¼ cup Pantry Dressing of your choice (pages 26–7)
¼ cup Honey Mustard Dressing (page 27)

PREP AHEAD

Brisket for Monday and Wednesday

2 Tablespoons olive oil

4 pounds beef brisket

1 teaspoon kosher salt

1 teaspoon black pepper

1 medium yellow onion, roughly chopped

2 garlic cloves, minced or pressed

2 Tablespoons tomato paste

4 cups low-sodium chicken or vegetable broth

1. Heat the oil in a Dutch oven or other heavy-bottomed pot over medium-high heat.
2. Season the brisket with the salt and pepper and sear on all sides until browned, about 10 minutes. Transfer the brisket to a plate and set aside.
3. Add the onion and garlic to the oil remaining in the pot and cook for 4 to 5 minutes, scraping the bottom of the pot with a wooden spatula to release the tasty bits. Stir in the tomato paste.
4. Place the meat over the onions, add the broth, and cover. Reduce the heat to low and cook the brisket for 2½ to 3 hours.
5. Let cool, then shred 2 pounds for Wednesday's lasagna; store the brisket in an airtight container in the refrigerator for dinner on Monday.

Fall Week II: Monday

AUNT JUDY'S BRISKET

with Roasted Potatoes

I'm not sure if this is exactly my aunt's version, but it's close enough to remind me of the holiday dinners around her table. It takes time to prepare a delicious braise, but it does not require constant attention. And cooking the brisket on Sunday gets you ready for two weeknight meals.

Serves 6: 1 hour  

for the roasted potatoes

2 pounds new potatoes, scrubbed

1 Tablespoon olive oil

½ teaspoon kosher salt

for the brisket

2 pounds Brisket (see Prep Ahead, page 154)

for the roasted potatoes

1. Preheat the oven to 350°F.
2. Toss the potatoes with the olive oil and salt. Arrange on a baking sheet and roast for about 45 minutes, turning once, until tender.
3. Serve alongside the reheated brisket.

for the brisket

Place in a saucepan with ½ cup water. Cover and heat on medium for about 5 minutes.

RATATOUILLE HALIBUT

with Basil Couscous

I can't make this dish without thinking about the little character in the Pixar movie of the same name. I have always believed "anyone can cook," and my kids now have that notion secured in their subconscious. Ratatouille is one of those dishes that just make families feel good. This recipe goes step by step so the vegetables don't turn red from the bell peppers.

Serves 4: 25 minutes 

for the ratatouille halibut

1 Tablespoon olive oil

½ yellow onion, chopped

2 garlic cloves, minced or pressed

1 zucchini, chopped

1 eggplant, chopped

1 red bell pepper, cored, seeded, and chopped

1¼ pounds halibut fillets (or any thick white-fleshed fish)

½ teaspoon kosher salt

½ teaspoon black pepper

¼ teaspoon sweet Hungarian paprika

2 Tablespoons grapeseed oil

for the basil couscous

1½ cups water

1 cup whole wheat couscous

1 Tablespoon olive oil

Grated zest and juice of ½ lemon

6 fresh basil leaves, shredded

½ teaspoon kosher salt

¼ teaspoon black pepper

for the ratatouille halibut

1. Heat the oil in a large sauté pan or skillet over medium heat. Add the onion and garlic and cook for 5 minutes, until translucent. Add the zucchini and cook for 3 minutes, until softened. Add the eggplant and cook for 3 minutes, until softened.
2. Add the bell pepper and cook for 4 to 5 minutes. Transfer the ratatouille mixture to a bowl; set the pan aside.
3. Season the fish with the salt, pepper, and paprika. Add the grapeseed oil to the pan. Once it is hot, add the fish to the pan and sear for 3 minutes.
4. Flip the fish over and cover with the ratatouille. Cover the pan and cook the fish for 5 minutes.
5. Remove the pan from the heat and let the fish steam for a few minutes, then serve.

for the basil couscous

1. Bring the water to a boil in a 2-quart saucepan. Stir in the couscous, cover the pan, and remove it from the heat. Let the couscous sit for 5 minutes.
2. Fluff the couscous with a fork. Mix in the olive oil, lemon zest and juice, basil, salt, and pepper.

 serve with brown rice instead of couscous

Fall Week II:
Tuesday

Fall Week II: Wednesday

BRAISED-BEEF SKILLET LASAGNA

with Green Salad

This is what I call lazy lasagna: it requires no labor-intensive layering and it cooks much faster. Made on the stovetop, it is perfect for a weeknight and hearty enough to comfort a hungry crowd.

Serves 5: 40 minutes

for the braised-beef skillet lasagna

- 1 Tablespoon grapeseed oil
- ½ yellow onion, chopped
- 2 garlic cloves, minced or pressed
- ⅓ cup tomato paste
- 2 Tablespoons dried oregano
- ½ teaspoon kosher salt
- 8 ounces whole wheat lasagna noodles, broken into 2-inch pieces
- 1 cup shredded mozzarella cheese
- 2 pounds shredded Brisket (see Prep Ahead, page 154)
- One 15-ounce can diced tomatoes, with juice
- 1 cup part-skim ricotta cheese or DIY Ricotta (pages 163–5)
- ¼ cup fresh basil leaves, torn into pieces

for the green salad

- 1 head red leaf lettuce, separated into leaves, washed, dried, and cut into bite-sized pieces
- 1 medium carrot, peeled and shredded
- 1 red bell pepper, cored, seeded, and thinly sliced
- ¼ cup Pantry Dressing of your choice (pages 26–7)

for the braised-beef skillet lasagna

1. Heat the oil in a medium sauté pan over medium-high heat. Add the onion and garlic and sauté for 3 to 4 minutes, until softened.
2. Mix in the tomato paste, stirring to coat the onions. Stir in the oregano and salt.
3. Arrange the noodle pieces in an even layer on top of the onions. Sprinkle the mozzarella over the noodles. Add the brisket to the pan over the noodles. Cover the meat layer with the tomatoes, including the juice.
4. Cook over medium heat for 15 to 20 minutes, until the noodles have absorbed the liquid and are soft.
5. Top the lasagna with a few dollops of the ricotta and sprinkle with the basil.

for the green salad

In a salad bowl, toss the lettuce with the shredded carrots and red bell pepper. Chill, then toss with the dressing or serve right away.

DIY
homemade ricotta

Ricotta is a versatile soft cheese made from curdled milk. Traditionally it is a by-product from making another cheese, but it is easy to make a version at home as a stand-alone product. I'll go out on a limb and declare that anything made at home is better for your health and happiness. Ricotta can be a quick, easy, and rewarding way to add homemade cheese to your repertoire of tricks. And the bragging rights on lasagna with homemade ricotta are priceless!

Yield: 3 cups

1 gallon organic whole milk (not ultrapasteurized)

⅓ cup fresh lemon juice

1 teaspoon kosher salt

Equipment

- Colander
- Cheesecloth
- Medium stockpot (nonreactive)
- Slotted spoon
- Kitchen string

1. Line a colander with a few layers of cheesecloth, making sure to leave a long overhang for lifting. Set it in a large bowl.

2. Combine the milk and lemon juice in a medium stockpot over medium-high heat until warm. Reduce the heat to medium and bring the milk to BARELY a simmer; do not allow it to boil. Remove the milk from the heat, add the salt, and set aside for 10 minutes; the milk will curdle.

3. With a slotted spoon, lift the curds from the milk and place them in the lined colander. Allow the curds to drain for 5 minutes.

4. Gather the edges of the cheesecloth up around the curds and tie them into a pouch with a long piece of string. Do not squeeze the ricotta, or you will remove moisture prematurely.

5. Hang the pouch over the end of a water spout or suspend it on a wooden spoon over a large pot. Drain for 15 to 20 minutes.

6. Store the ricotta in an airtight container in the refrigerator for up to 4 days. Ricotta is best when fresh!

Tips

- Use organic nonhomogenized milk.
- Make sure the milk does not come to a boil; this will create an undesirable rubbery texture.
- Do not stir the heated milk. Let the milk curdle on its own.
- Do not squeeze the ricotta to remove excess water; let it drain on its own.

Add-ins

- Grated lemon zest
- Herbes de Provence

Serving Ideas

- Spread over tomato slices.
- Add a healthy dollop to pasta.
- Use instead of mozzarella on homemade pizza.
- Sweeten with a little honey and serve with granola.

SPLIT PEA AND HAM SOUP

with Crunchy Fall Salad

Dried legumes can sometimes be intimidating. Have no fear, these little green wonders are extremely simple to prepare. You just might leave canned soup behind for good.

Serves 4–5: 55 minutes  

for the split pea and ham soup

2 Tablespoons olive oil

1 medium yellow onion, chopped

2 medium carrots, peeled and chopped

1 celery stalk, chopped

½ teaspoon kosher salt, plus more to taste

2 garlic cloves, minced or pressed

8 cups water

1 pound lean ham (about a 1-inch-thick slice from the deli)

2 cups dried split peas, picked through to remove any dirt or rocks

1 Tablespoon fresh thyme leaves

Black pepper to taste

for the crunchy fall salad

1 head red leaf lettuce, separated into leaves, torn into pieces, washed, and dried

⅓ cup hazelnuts, toasted and skins removed

1 celery stalk, chopped

¼ cup Honey Mustard Dressing (page 27)

for the split pea and ham soup

1. Heat the oil in a large Dutch oven over medium heat. When the oil is hot, add the onion, carrots, and celery, season with the salt, and cook, stirring frequently, until softened, 3 to 4 minutes. Add the garlic and cook until fragrant, about 30 seconds.

2. Add the water, ham, peas, and thyme, increase the heat to high, and bring the soup to a simmer, stirring frequently to keep the peas from sticking to the bottom of the pot. Reduce the heat to low, cover, and simmer until the peas are tender but not falling apart, about 45 minutes.

3. Turn off the heat and remove the ham from the soup. Cover it with foil or plastic wrap to prevent it from drying out, and let cool.

4. When it is cool enough to handle, shred the ham into small bite-sized pieces using two forks. Stir the ham back into soup and return the soup to a simmer. Season to taste with black pepper.

for the crunchy fall salad

In a medium salad bowl, combine the lettuce, hazelnuts, and celery. Toss with the dressing to taste.

Fall Week II: Thursday

Fall Week II: Friday

EGGPLANT CAPONATA PENNE

I love everything about this dinner. The salty-sweet flavors of the simmered vegetables combined with the creamy ricotta and the earthy pasta make for a soul-satisfying experience. And who doesn't love a one-bowl meal?

Serves 4: 30 minutes 

for the eggplant caponata

3 Tablespoons olive oil

1 medium yellow onion, diced

1 pound eggplant, cut into ½-inch pieces (the smaller the pieces, the quicker the skin will become soft while cooking)

3 garlic cloves, minced or pressed

One 15-ounce can diced tomatoes

1 cup low-sodium chicken or vegetable broth

1 red bell pepper, cored, seeded, and diced

2 Tablespoons balsamic vinegar

¼ cup loosely packed fresh basil leaves, roughly chopped

2 teaspoons dried oregano

½ teaspoon kosher salt

½ teaspoon black pepper

for the pasta

8 ounces whole wheat penne

½ cup part-skim ricotta cheese or DIY Ricotta (pages 163–5)

for the eggplant caponata

1. Heat a large nonstick sauté pan over medium heat. Add the olive oil. Once it is hot, add the onion and eggplant and cook, stirring often, for 4 to 5 minutes, until soft.

2. Add the garlic, tomatoes, broth, bell pepper, balsamic vinegar, basil, oregano, salt, and pepper, stirring to combine, then reduce the heat to medium-low and simmer for 15 to 20 minutes.

for the pasta

1. Bring a large pot of salted water to a boil. Add the pasta and cook until al dente, about 9 minutes; drain.

2. Serve the penne topped with the warm caponata and garnished with a dollop of the ricotta cheese.

FALL MENU

MONDAY

Muffin Tin Meatloaf
with Broccoli Forest Rice

TUESDAY

Shrimp Gumbo

WEDNESDAY

Chicken Tamale Spoon Bread

THURSDAY

Spaghetti and Meatballs

FRIDAY

Broccoli Cheddar Soup
with No-Waste Leftovers

SHOPPING LIST

Meat/Seafood

2 pounds lean ground beef or turkey

1 pound shrimp in the shell

2 boneless, skinless chicken breasts (about 1¼ pounds)

Note: Extra-lean beef results in a dryer loaf; I use an 85/15 mix of ground beef or turkey.

Vegetables/Fruit

4 medium onions

3 medium carrots

1 medium green bell pepper

2 cups frozen corn

3 heads broccoli

2 celery stalks

½ bunch fresh flat-leaf parsley

Dairy

4 large eggs

2½ cups 2% milk

1½ cups shredded cheddar cheese

1 cup grated Parmesan cheese

3 Tablespoons unsalted butter

Bakery/Misc.

2 whole wheat dinner rolls, bakery fresh

One 15-ounce can diced tomatoes

One 32-ounce can diced tomatoes

1 cup cornmeal

From the Pantry

6¾ teaspoons kosher salt

2¼ teaspoons black pepper

1½ teaspoons cayenne pepper

1 Tablespoon dried oregano

1 teaspoon ground cumin

¾ teaspoon sweet Hungarian paprika

2 Tablespoons olive oil

¼ cup plus 2 Tablespoons grapeseed oil

8 garlic cloves

1 Tablespoon plus 2 teaspoons Dijon mustard

2 teaspoons reduced-sodium soy sauce

6 ounces plus 2 Tablespoons tomato paste

2 Tablespoons honey

2½ cups brown rice (dry)

10 cups low-sodium chicken or vegetable broth

12 ounces whole wheat spaghetti

2 Tablespoons whole wheat flour

PREP AHEAD

Meatloaf Mix for Monday and Thursday

- 2 pounds lean ground beef or turkey
- 1 cup bread crumbs (see below)
- 3 Tablespoons chopped fresh flat-leaf parsley
- 1½ medium onions, chopped
- 2 medium carrots, shredded
- 2 large eggs
- 2 teaspoons Dijon mustard
- 2 teaspoons reduced-sodium soy sauce
- 1½ teaspoons kosher salt
- 1 teaspoon black pepper

1. In a large bowl, combine the meat, bread crumbs, parsley, onions, carrots, eggs, Dijon, soy sauce, salt, and pepper until well mixed. Don't be afraid to use your hands. Kids can have fun with this!
2. Remove half of the meatloaf mix and store in an airtight container in the refrigerator for dinner on Thursday. Freeze if necessary.
3. Divide the remaining meatloaf mixture into 12 equal portions and shape into balls. Press the balls down into lightly greased muffin cups. Or, if you don't have a muffin pan, form the mixture into 4 individual loaves and place on a baking sheet. Cover the pan with plastic wrap and store in the refrigerator until dinner on Monday night.

for the bread crumbs

- 2 whole wheat dinner rolls, bakery fresh

1. Cut rolls into slices that will fit into the toaster.
2. Toast until crisp. Let cool.
3. Grind in a food processor or blender until mealy crumbs are formed.
4. Store in an airtight container for up to a week.

Yield: 1 cup

Brown Rice for Monday and Tuesday

Prepare 5 cups brown rice (see page xvii)

mince, dice, and chop

There are so many fancy names for the way vegetables are cut, and as a home cook, it's not necessary to keep up with the foundations of professional French cooking. I'm not going to talk about a ***brunoise*** cut, because for weeknight meals in my kitchen, it's never going to happen. For our purposes, everything is referenced by mince, dice, and chop.

Fall Week III: Monday

MUFFIN TIN MEATLOAF

with Broccoli Forest Rice

Weeknights need to move fast, and meatloaf can take forever in a loaf pan. I make these mini versions ahead of time and pop them in the oven for 15 minutes on dinner night. A simple blend of tomato paste, mustard, and honey eliminates the need for a traditional ketchup topping. The presentation of a broccoli tree forest adds fun to a traditional family meal. This dinner is a sure hit with the under-ten crowd.

Serves 5: 25 minutes

for the muffin tin meatloaf

- 1 pound Meatloaf Mix in a muffin pan (see Prep Ahead, page 172)
- 2 Tablespoons tomato paste
- 1 Tablespoon Dijon mustard
- 2 Tablespoons honey

for the broccoli forest rice

- 1 head broccoli, broken into floret pieces with 2 inches of stem attached
- 2 cups prepared brown rice
- 1 medium carrot, shredded
- ¼ teaspoon sweet Hungarian paprika
- ¼ teaspoon kosher salt
- ¼ teaspoon black pepper

for the muffin tin meatloaf

1. Preheat the oven to 400°F. Remove the muffin pan from the fridge and remove the plastic wrap.
2. In a small bowl, mix the tomato paste, Dijon, and honey. Baste the tops of the meatloaves with the mixture.
3. Bake for about 15 minutes, until the meat mixture is firm but moist; the internal temperature should be 165°F. If using turkey, it will take an extra 7 minutes.

for the broccoli forest rice

1. Place the broccoli in a 2-quart saucepan with ½ cup water.
2. Cover and steam on medium heat for 3 to 4 minutes. Do not overcook.
3. Remove from heat and strain.
4. In the same saucepan, heat 2 cups of prepared rice with 1 Tablespoon water over medium heat until warmed through.
5. Arrange rice on a large plate.
6. Place broccoli "trees" standing up in the rice to form a "forest" in the rice.
7. Sprinkle shredded carrot on the edges of the plate.
8. Dust with paprika, salt, and pepper before presenting at the dinner table.

SHRIMP GUMBO

This recipe proves that it is possible to make a quick, satisfying weeknight version of traditional slow-cooked gumbo. If you like, double the cayenne to increase the heat. My Auntie Neats would be proud!

Serves 5: 25 minutes

- 2 Tablespoons grapeseed oil
- 2 Tablespoons whole wheat flour
- 1 medium onion, minced
- 2 celery stalks, minced
- 2 garlic cloves, minced or pressed
- 1 teaspoon ground cumin
- ½ teaspoon cayenne pepper
- ½ teaspoon sweet Hungarian paprika
- 4 cups low-sodium chicken or vegetable broth
- 1 pound shrimp, peeled and deveined
- 3 cups prepared brown rice
- ¼ cup chopped fresh flat-leaf parsley

1. Heat a large skillet over high heat. Add the oil and flour to the pan and whisk together quickly. Cook, whisking, until the mixture is well blended and starts to brown. Stir in the onion, celery, and garlic until well coated. Cook for 3 to 4 minutes.
2. Season with the cumin, cayenne, and paprika.
3. Pour in the broth, cover, and simmer for 15 minutes.
4. Stir in the shrimp. Add the brown rice, stir, and heat through for 3 to 4 minutes, until the shrimp is opaque.
5. Divide the gumbo among bowls and garnish with the parsley.

Fall Week III: Tuesday

CHICKEN TAMALE SPOON BREAD

Now this is what I call supper: hearty ingredients stewed together, with a sweet, cheesy cornmeal topping. I named the recipe spoon bread because my family eats it straight from the pan with spoons. Isn't that what sharing is about?

Serves 4–6: 45 minutes 

for the spoon bread

¼ cup grapeseed oil

1 medium onion, chopped

1 medium green bell pepper, cored, seeded, and chopped

1 garlic clove, minced or pressed

2 boneless, skinless chicken breasts, cut into 1-inch cubes (about 1¼ pounds)

One 15-ounce can diced tomatoes

2 cups frozen corn

1 teaspoon kosher salt

1 teaspoon cayenne pepper

½ teaspoon black pepper

½ cup cornmeal

1 cup water

for the topping

2½ cups 2% milk

2 Tablespoons unsalted butter

½ teaspoon kosher salt

½ cup cornmeal

1 cup shredded cheddar cheese

2 large eggs, beaten

for the spoon bread

1. Preheat the oven to 375°F.
2. Heat the oil in a medium sauté pan over medium heat. Add the onions, green pepper, and garlic and sauté until the onions are golden. Add the chicken and cook, stirring, for about 4 minutes to sear on all sides.
3. Stir in the tomatoes, corn, salt, cayenne, and black pepper, cover, and simmer for 5 minutes.
4. Whisk in the cornmeal blended with the water and simmer for 10 minutes longer. Pour the mixture into a 9-x-13-inch baking dish.

for the topping

1. Combine the milk with the butter and salt in a 2-quart saucepan, and heat over medium-low heat, until it just begins to simmer; do not boil. Gradually stir in the cornmeal and cook, stirring, until thickened but not stiff.
2. Remove the pan from the heat and stir in the cheese and eggs. Spread the topping over the chicken mixture in the baking dish. Bake, uncovered, for 20 minutes, until the cheese is golden brown.

"AN INVALUABLE RESOURCE."

— Dawn

Q: Why did you purchase a subscription to The Fresh 20?

A: I had been wanting to sign up for about six months but just hadn't done it. Then our holistic doctor said that we needed to go gluten free because of my daughter's autoimmune arthritis and mixed connective tissue disease. Feeling completely overwhelmed, I *knew* that The Fresh 20 was going to play a key role in helping me navigate this new lifestyle!

Q: What were your family's eating habits like before joining The Fresh 20?

A: About three years ago, we started on a sugar-free, mostly dairy-free journey (they are both big inflammatory foods). Up until a few months ago, I would allow artificial sweeteners and processed foods. When we decided to add holistic/alternative treatments to our daughter's regimen, I got serious about feeding her fresh whole foods.

Q: Please share with us a family memory that involves the kitchen.

A: I've always been more of a baker than a cook. From an early age, my daughter loved baking cakes with me. She would decorate them and then we would surprise her cousins on their birthdays. Now that we are eating healthier, we are working on finding a birthday cake recipe that tastes good and fits her dietary restrictions for *her* birthday this year!

We also love to do our own version of *Food Network Challenge*/*Iron Chef* where we create plates from set ingredients. At seven, Sadie is *all* about presentation!

Q: How has The Fresh 20 changed your family?

A: Making the commitment to be gluten free was daunting, to say the least. I feel like a Martha Stewart wannabe because I am in my kitchen constantly! It is overwhelming enough without having to sift and search online for new recipes. Knowing that The Fresh 20 will deliver new recipes to my in-box each week has been like having a reliable, supportive friend walking with me on this new journey. Even though I often have to tweak the recipes to be sugar free and dairy free, The Fresh 20 has been an INVALUABLE resource. We've found several new favorites that consistently make it into the rotation.

DENNIS, 49

DAWN, 44

SADIE, 7

SPAGHETTI AND MEATBALLS

I couldn't write a family cookbook without the king of pasta dishes. While the slow-cooked tomato sauces of the weekend are divine, this version takes very little time. It's really hard not to eat the entire platter.

Serves 6: 35 minutes

for the meatballs

1 pound Meatloaf Mix (see Prep Ahead, page 172)

2 garlic cloves, minced or pressed

1 Tablespoon dried oregano

for the spaghetti

6 ounces tomato paste

2 garlic cloves, minced or pressed

3 teaspoons kosher salt

One 32-ounce can diced tomatoes

2 cups low-sodium chicken or vegetable broth

12 ounces whole wheat spaghetti

1 Tablespoon olive oil

1 Tablespoon unsalted butter, melted

2 Tablespoons finely chopped fresh flat-leaf parsley

1 cup grated Parmesan cheese

for the meatballs

1. Preheat the oven to 350°F.
2. Using clean hands, combine the meatloaf mix, garlic, and oregano.
3. Divide the mixture into 12 portions and shape into meatballs. Arrange the meatballs in a lightly greased baking dish large enough to hold them without touching.
4. Bake the meatballs for 25 minutes, until cooked through. (You can also panfry the meatballs on the stovetop in 1 Tablespoon olive oil in a large skillet, turning frequently so they cook evenly.)

for the spaghetti

1. Meanwhile, combine the tomato paste, garlic, and 1 teaspoon of the salt in a large saucepan over medium-high heat and cook for 3 to 4 minutes, until the paste has darkened. Add the tomatoes and broth, bring to a simmer, and simmer for 10 minutes.
2. Bring a large pot of water to a boil and add the remaining 2 teaspoons of the salt. Add the pasta and cook until al dente. Drain; do not rinse. Transfer to a large bowl.
3. Immediately toss the pasta with the olive oil and butter. Mix in the parsley. Fold in the Parmesan. Add the tomato sauce, stir, and serve the pasta with the meatballs.

Fall Week III: Thursday

Fall Week III: Friday

BROCCOLI CHEDDAR SOUP

with No-Waste Leftovers

Broccoli is often a symbol for all vegetables: kids either love it or they hate it. This simple soup is my answer for picky eaters. It's creamy, cheesy, and full of healthy vegetables. If you roast broccoli, it releases a nutty flavor. This recipe is for a puree soup, which is thicker and chunkier than cream soups. Adjust the texture according to preference by increasing the milk as desired.

Serves 4: 20 minutes  

- 1 Tablespoon olive oil
- ½ onion, roughly chopped
- 2 heads broccoli, stems and florets chopped
- 1 garlic clove, cut in half
- ½ teaspoon kosher salt
- ½ teaspoon black pepper
- 4 cups low-sodium chicken or vegetable broth
- ½ cup grated cheddar cheese

1. Heat the oil in a 5-quart Dutch oven or other heavy pot over medium heat. Add the onion and sauté until tender, about 4 minutes.
2. Add the broccoli, garlic, salt, and pepper and cook for 3 to 4 minutes. Add the broth and bring the soup to a simmer. Remove from the heat.
3. Transfer the soup to a blender or food processor in batches and puree until smooth. Return the soup to the pot, bring to a simmer, and simmer for 3 minutes.
4. Just before serving, fold in the cheese.
5. Serve with the week's leftovers for a waste-free week.

FALL MENU WEEK 4

MONDAY
Newlywed Macaroni and Cheese
with Side Salad

TUESDAY
Sweetheart Scallops
with Spinach Rice Medley

WEDNESDAY
Pumpkin Shepherd's Pie
with Cranberry Salad

THURSDAY
Mom's Midwest Goulash

FRIDAY
Pumpkin Hash
with Italian Turkey Sausage and Sage Corn

SHOPPING LIST

Meat/Seafood

1½ pounds Italian turkey sausage (preferably bulk sausage)
1¼ pounds bay scallops
2 pounds lean ground turkey or beef

Vegetables/Fruit

One 4-pound pumpkin
3 medium onions
7 medium carrots
1 head romaine lettuce, chopped
12 fresh sage leaves
One 1-inch piece of fresh ginger
½ cup grape or cherry tomatoes
4 cups frozen corn
14 cups baby spinach (1½ pounds)
4 large Yukon Gold potatoes

Dairy

3 cups 2% milk
3 large egg whites
5 Tablespoons unsalted butter
3 cups shredded cheddar cheese
1 cup shredded Monterey Jack cheese

Bakery/Misc.

One 14½-ounce can diced tomatoes
½ cup dried cranberries
¼ cup chopped nuts (walnuts, hazelnuts, or your choice)

From the Pantry

4¼ teaspoons kosher salt
1 teaspoon black pepper
½ teaspoon cayenne pepper
¾ teaspoon ground cumin
1 teaspoon sweet Hungarian paprika
¼ cup olive oil
6 garlic cloves
3½ cups low-sodium chicken or vegetable broth
¼ cup Pantry Dressing of your choice (pages 26–7)
⅓ cup whole wheat flour
1½ cups brown rice (dry)
1½ pounds whole wheat macaroni
Two 6-ounce cans tomato paste

PREP AHEAD

Roasted Pumpkin for Wednesday and Friday

One 4-pound pumpkin, cut in half and seeds removed

1 Tablespoon olive oil

1. Preheat the oven to 350°F.
2. Brush the cut sides of the pumpkin with the olive oil and place the pumpkin flesh side down in a baking dish. Pour in ¼ inch of water and bake for 45 to 60 minutes, until the pumpkin flesh is tender. Let cool.
3. Scoop out the flesh from one half of the pumpkin. Store in an airtight container in the refrigerator for dinner on Wednesday.
4. Peel and cube the remaining pumpkin. Store in an airtight container in the refrigerator for dinner on Friday.

Brown Rice for Tuesday

Prepare 3 cups brown rice (see page xvii).

a fresh idea:

TREAT YOURSELF

Cooking delicious food on a budget has become a welcome challenge every week. The idea of The Fresh 20 is less is more, which means that I save on everyday cooking. As a reward for my savings, I treat myself to something divine on the weekend. An aged balsamic vinegar or an over-the-top fresh pasta is a good candidate, along with this list of some well-worth-it ingredient splurges. Go ahead and indulge. You deserve it!

My favorite quality ingredients:

- A prime cut of meat
- Special sea salt
- Organic chocolate
- Artisanal cheese
- Freshly roasted coffee from an independent roaster
- Fancy nuts
- A bottle of wine from a specialty wine store

pantry dinners

Every household needs a back-up plan. Having a handful of recipes that can be created from a limited pantry can be a lifesaver. When a day has failed me and I am overtired or stressed, my go-to dinner is scrambled eggs with pasta. No eggs? Pasta with olive oil, garlic, dried oregano, and Parmesan. No pasta? Brown rice or canned beans. You get the picture. Sometimes dinner is hiding in the cabinet. I call these Pantry Dinners.

Pantry Chili

1 can beans (any variety)

1 can diced tomatoes

2 cups prepared brown rice

Mix together and heat to a simmer.

Pantry Omelet

6 large eggs

¼ cup cheese (any variety)

2 Tablespoons water

½ teaspoon kosher salt

1 teaspoon any dried herb

Whisk together and bake at 350°F for 20 minutes.

Fall Week IV: Monday

NEWLYWED MACARONI AND CHEESE

with Side Salad

When I was first married, I created a "homemade" meal using *that* box of the cheesiest mac and cheese. You know, the one with the bright neon coloring? I would remove gourmet Italian sausage from its casings and mix the meat with the orange macaroni, set the table, and call my husband to dinner. It was his favorite dish. This is the grown-up, whole-food version, which still wins his heart today. Try a good Italian market for fresh bulk sausage. If you get links, remove the casings and carry on.

Serves 5: 25 minutes

for the macaroni and cheese

1½ teaspoons kosher salt

12 ounces whole wheat macaroni

1 pound Italian turkey sausage, removed from casings if necessary

3 Tablespoons unsalted butter

½ medium onion, finely chopped

2 garlic cloves, minced or pressed

⅓ cup whole wheat flour

3 cups 2% milk

¼ teaspoon black pepper

¼ teaspoon sweet Hungarian paprika

3 cups shredded cheddar cheese

½ cup shredded Monterey Jack cheese

for the side salad

1 medium carrot, peeled and shredded

4 cups chopped romaine lettuce

2 Tablespoons Pantry Dressing of your choice (pages 26–7)

for the macaroni and cheese

1. Bring a large pot of water to a boil. Add 1 teaspoon of the salt, then add the pasta and cook until al dente. Drain the pasta; do not rinse.
2. Meanwhile, brown the sausage in a 5-quart Dutch oven or other heavy pot over medium heat. Transfer the meat to a bowl and set aside.
3. Add the butter, onion, and garlic to the pot and sauté until the onions are softened, about 4 minutes. Stir in the flour and cook, stirring for 2 minutes, or until the raw flour smell is gone.
4. Pour in the milk, stirring, and bring to a simmer. Season with the remaining ½ teaspoon salt, the pepper, and the paprika. Stir in the cheeses until melted. Cover the pot and set aside until the pasta is done.
5. Combine the pasta with the cheese sauce. Fold in the sausage and serve immediately with the side salad.

for the side salad

In a medium salad bowl, toss all the ingredients together until well mixed.

SWEETHEART SCALLOPS

with Spinach Rice Medley

All three of my "boys" love scallops. I prepare this dish to make them feel special, and it comforts me to know it will also make them strong—like Popeye, only cuter. Medium bay scallops, in my opinion, have the mildest, nuttiest flavor.

Serves 4: 20 minutes 

for the scallops

1¼ pounds bay scallops

2 Tablespoons unsalted butter

1 Tablespoon olive oil

8 fresh sage leaves

1 garlic clove, minced or pressed

for the spinach rice medley

8 cups baby spinach

3 cups prepared brown rice

½ cup grape or cherry tomatoes

1 cup frozen corn

½ cup low-sodium chicken or vegetable broth

for the scallops

1. Rinse and pat dry the scallops.
2. Melt the butter with the olive oil in a large skillet over medium heat.
3. Sauté the sage and garlic for 1 minute.
4. Arrange the scallops, flat side down, in the pan and cook for about 2 to 3 minutes on each side, until they are opaque.

for the spinach rice medley

1. Combine the spinach, rice, tomatoes, and corn in a large pot. Pour in the broth, bring to a simmer over medium heat, and cook until the corn is tender and the liquid has evaporated, about 5 minutes.
2. Arrange the rice on a serving platter and place the scallops over the rice to serve.

Fall Week IV: Tuesday

frozen vegetables

I'm committed to keeping it fresh in the grocery department, but there are times when availability and quality dictate the need for a frozen alternative. I lean toward a limited selection of frozen fruits and vegetables to complete an otherwise produce-deficient meal. Many frozen vegetables are picked at their peak when nutrients are still intact, and research has shown that high-quality frozen vegetables can be more nutrient-packed than produce picked underripe to be shipped to your local supermarket. Choose the highest grade available, USDA "U.S. Fancy," and stay away from brands that add sodium. Just defrost, steam, and serve.

My frozen list:

- Corn
- Sweet peas
- Artichoke hearts
- Edamame
- Green beans

PUMPKIN SHEPHERD'S PIE

with Cranberry Salad

This sweet, light soufflé with the flavors of Thanksgiving makes a windy autumn night feel nostalgic. Similar to a shepherd's pie, this version has a surprising and delicious twist—the meaty filling is topped with airy mashed pumpkin instead of potatoes.

Serves 4–5: 45 minutes  

for the filling

- 1 Tablespoon olive oil
- ½ medium onion, roughly chopped
- 3 garlic cloves, minced
- One 1-inch piece of fresh ginger, grated
- 2 medium carrots, peeled and chopped
- ½ teaspoon ground cumin
- ½ teaspoon kosher salt
- ¼ teaspoon black pepper
- ¼ teaspoon sweet paprika
- 1 pound lean ground turkey or beef
- 2 cups baby spinach

for the topping

- 3 large egg whites
- Flesh from ½ Roasted Pumpkin (see Prep Ahead, page 188), mashed (about 2 cups)
- ¼ teaspoon cayenne pepper
- ¼ teaspoon kosher salt

for the cranberry salad

- ½ cup dried cranberries
- 4 cups baby spinach
- ¼ cup chopped nuts (walnuts, hazelnuts, or your choice)
- 2 Tablespoons Pantry Dressing of your choice (pages 26–7)

for the filling

1. Preheat the oven to 350°F.
2. Heat the oil in a medium skillet over medium-high heat. Add the onion, garlic, ginger, and carrots and sauté until slightly browned, about 5 minutes. Season with the cumin, salt, pepper, and paprika.
3. Add the ground meat and brown until no longer pink.
4. Toss in the baby spinach to wilt and transfer to a greased 8-x-8-inch baking dish.

for the topping

1. Using a handheld mixer, whisk the egg whites in a large bowl until stiff.
2. In a medium bowl, combine the pumpkin with the cayenne and salt. Fold in the egg whites.
3. Spread the topping over the filling. Bake for 20 minutes, until golden on top.

for the cranberry salad

Toss all the ingredients together in a medium bowl. Chill and serve.

MOM'S MIDWEST GOULASH

Midwestern goulash was in heavy rotation in my childhood home. To my mom, goulash meant canned tomatoes, ground beef, and noodles mixed with a never-ending parade of dried spices and herbs—as long as paprika was included, she called it goulash. My The Fresh 20 version stays pretty close to the original. Feel free to experiment with different flavors from your pantry; this basic recipe is perfect for customizing.

Serves 4–5: 20 minutes

- 1½ teaspoons kosher salt
- 12 ounces whole wheat macaroni
- 1 Tablespoon olive oil
- 1 medium onion, diced
- 1 pound lean ground turkey or beef
- ½ teaspoon black pepper
- ½ teaspoon sweet Hungarian paprika
- Two 6-ounce cans tomato paste
- One 14½-ounce can diced tomatoes
- 2 cups low-sodium chicken or vegetable broth
- 1 cup frozen corn
- ½ cup shredded Monterey Jack cheese
- 4 medium carrots, peeled and cut into sticks

1. Bring a large pot of water to a boil and add 1 teaspoon of the salt. Add the pasta and cook until al dente; drain.
2. Meanwhile, heat the oil in a large 5-quart Dutch oven or other heavy-bottomed pot over medium heat. Add the onion and sauté until soft, stirring frequently. Remove the onion and set aside.
3. Add the ground meat to the pot and brown it. Season with the remaining ½ teaspoon salt, the pepper, and the paprika. Stir in the tomato paste, then add the onions, tomatoes, and broth and bring to a simmer.
4. Mix in the pasta and corn. Top the goulash with the shredded cheese. Cover the pot and let sit for about 5 minutes.
5. Serve with the carrot sticks.

GF sub gluten-free pasta and broth

omit cheese

Fall Week IV: Thursday

Fall Week IV: Friday

PUMPKIN HASH

with Italian Turkey Sausage and Sage Corn

For years, I relegated pumpkin to a Halloween and pie-only ingredient, but recently I discovered that sweet pumpkin goes really well in savory dishes. Canned pumpkin won't work in this recipe, but any autumn squash will substitute nicely.

Serves 4: 30 minutes  

for the pumpkin hash

½ pound Italian turkey sausage, removed from casings if necessary

1 medium onion, finely chopped

4 large Yukon Gold potatoes, peeled and chopped into ½-inch cubes

1 cup low-sodium chicken or vegetable broth

½ teaspoon kosher salt

¼ teaspoon cayenne pepper

¼ teaspoon ground cumin

Cubed Roasted Pumpkin (see Prep Ahead, page 188), about 2 cups

for the sage corn

2 cups frozen corn

4 fresh sage leaves, minced

for the pumpkin hash

1. Brown the sausage in a large skillet over medium heat until thoroughly cooked. Transfer the sausage to a bowl, reserving the fat in the pan.
2. Add the onion to the pan and sauté until soft, about 4 minutes.
3. Add the potatoes, broth, and seasonings, cover, and simmer for 6 to 8 minutes, until the potatoes are fork-tender.
4. Add the reserved sausage and the cubed pumpkin and cook until the potatoes begin to brown, about 10 minutes.

for the sage corn

In a small 1-quart saucepan, heat the corn for 3 minutes, or until warmed through. Stir in the sage.

IN SEASON

- Bok choy
- Brussels sprouts
- Butternut squash
- Carrots
- Collard greens
- Fennel
- Mushrooms
- Oranges
- Parsley
- Parsnips
- Pears
- Pomegranates
- Sweet potatoes
- Tangerines
- Tomatillos

WINTER

Winter was epic in Minnesota. The cold front moved in around Thanksgiving, and while fun at first—snow angels, sledding, ice-skating and hot chocolate—by Christmas it became an ordeal to suit up like a Michelin Tire man every time we needed to leave the house.

Winter cooking is more work as well. Thick-skinned vegetables like butternut squash and pumpkin take more time to prepare. Winter is magical even with the harshness of the season and the extra prep required.

The oven gets quite a workout in the winter. The flavorful, economical cuts of meat—brisket, shanks, pot roast, pork loin—are wonderful braised in the traditional way: cooked slowly in liquid in the oven (or the Crock-Pot).

When I was growing up, my family convened most frequently for meals in winter. With bitter cold wind and snow falling, indoors was the only place to gather. Sitting in the kitchen near the oven was the best place to catch the warmth. More than any other season, winter draws family together around the dinner table.

Where I live, in mostly sunny California, there are not many clues to tell you it's winter. No leaves turning color, no promise of a white blanket of holiday snow. I take my cue from the food. Winter's produce guides my sensibilities: the durability of winter vegetables and the simple but necessary techniques to break them down into soft, fragrant, satisfying meals.

I believe happiness begins in the kitchen and the warmth of a family can be traced back to those memories made when it is cold outside and the oven is hot. I have a warm family. Winter is their time to be nourished. These weeknight dinners are meant to comfort like a big hug from my kitchen. I hope your family will feel the love.

WINTER MENU

WEEK 1

MONDAY

Crock-Pot Roast with Braised Carrots and Parsnips

TUESDAY

Maple-Soy Salmon with Bok Choy and Brown Rice

WEDNESDAY

Vegetable Minestrone

THURSDAY

Spicy Beef Farfalle

FRIDAY

Fancy Franks and Beans

SHOPPING LIST

Meat/Seafood

One 2½- to 3-pound boneless beef chuck roast
1¼ pounds salmon fillets (4 fillets)
1½ pounds chicken or Italian turkey sausage links

Vegetables/Fruit

8 medium carrots
5 medium parsnips
2 pounds baby bok choy
2 pints grape or cherry tomatoes
3½ medium yellow onions
4 celery stalks
6 fresh sage leaves
2 medium zucchini
2 medium yellow summer squash
2 small fresh red Thai chile peppers
2 medium cucumbers
One 1-inch piece fresh ginger

Dairy

1 cup Parmesan cheese, plus a 3-inch Parmesan rind

Bakery/Misc.

Four 14-ounce cans cannellini beans

From the Pantry

4 teaspoons kosher salt
2¼ teaspoons black pepper
1½ teaspoons ground cumin
½ teaspoon sweet Hungarian paprika
¾ teaspoon cayenne pepper
1 teaspoon dried oregano
3 Tablespoons grapeseed oil
14 cups low-sodium chicken or vegetable broth
½ cup pure maple syrup
¼ cup reduced-sodium soy sauce
4 garlic cloves
6 Tablespoons olive oil
1 Tablespoon balsamic vinegar
One 6-ounce can tomato paste
1 pound whole wheat farfalle (or other short pasta, like penne, ziti, or rigatoni)
1 cup brown rice (dry)

Winter Week 1:
Monday

CROCK-POT ROAST

with Braised Carrots and Parsnips

Pot roast was one of my favorite dishes in my mother's limited repertoire. She would prepare it on one of the many cold winter weekends in Minnesota. It was an inexpensive but hearty way to celebrate Sunday supper with family. Inspired by my mom's recipe, my weeknight version includes parsnips instead of potatoes for a surprising, fragrant twist. Sage, earthy and pungent, balances the sweetness of the parsnips. Pot roast is comfort food at the core.

Serves 4–5: 5 hours  

- 2 teaspoons kosher salt
- 1 teaspoon black pepper
- 1 teaspoon ground cumin
- ½ teaspoon cayenne pepper
- ½ teaspoon sweet Hungarian paprika
- One 2½- to 3-pound boneless beef chuck roast
- 2 Tablespoons grapeseed oil
- 1 medium yellow onion, roughly chopped
- 5 medium carrots, peeled and sliced lengthwise in half
- 4 medium parsnips, peeled and sliced lengthwise in half
- 2 celery stalks, trimmed and cut in half
- 6 fresh sage leaves, chopped
- 4 cups low-sodium chicken or vegetable broth

Note: If you do not have a Crock-Pot, use a Dutch oven or other heavy, ovenproof pot to brown the meat, then add the vegetables, sage, and broth, cover, and cook in a 275°F oven for 3 hours.

1. Combine the salt, black pepper, cumin, cayenne pepper, and paprika in a small bowl. Rub the seasonings into the meat on all sides.

2. In a large skillet, heat the grapeseed oil over medium-high heat. Once the oil sizzles, place the meat in the pan and sear on all sides until a brown crust forms, about 5 minutes per side.

3. Place the vegetables and sage in the bottom of a Crock-Pot. Arrange the browned meat on the bed of vegetables. Pour in the broth. Set the Crock-Pot to low if cooking for more than 5 hours, or high if cooking for 3 to 5 hours. Cover the Crock-Pot and leave to cook.

Note: Only check on it when you think the meat is close to being finished. Each time the lid is removed, the temperature drops dramatically.

Leftover Note: Slice off a 1-pound piece of the roast. Store the meat in an airtight container in the refrigerator for dinner on Thursday.

MAPLE–SOY SALMON

with Bok Choy and Brown Rice

Salmon has never been my favorite fish, but it is always requested by my husband and kids—not to mention the wonderful health benefits it provides. Pure 100 percent maple syrup is the key to the recipe's success. The vibrant green leaves and crunchy stalks of bok choy, which you can find year-round in most markets, are a great complement to the tender salty-sweet salmon.

Serves 4: 20 minutes  

- 1 Tablespoon grapeseed oil
- ½ cup pure maple syrup
- ¼ cup reduced-sodium soy sauce or gluten-free tamari
- 2 garlic cloves, minced or pressed
- 1 Tablespoon grated fresh ginger
- ¼ teaspoon cayenne pepper
- 1¼ pounds salmon fillets (4 fillets)
- ¼ teaspoon kosher salt
- ¼ teaspoon black pepper
- 1 pound baby bok choy, halved
- 1 Tablespoon olive oil
- 2 cups prepared brown rice

1. Place a rack 5 inches from the heat and preheat the broiler. Line a baking sheet with aluminum foil and brush with the grapeseed oil. (This helps with cleanup!)

2. Whisk the syrup, soy sauce, garlic, ginger, and cayenne together in a small saucepan. Bring to a simmer over medium heat and simmer for 5 to 7 minutes, until the sauce is as thick as syrup. Set aside to cool.

3. Arrange the salmon on the broiler pan and season with the salt and pepper. Surround the fish with the bok choy and brush with olive oil. Place the pan under the broiler and broil for 5 minutes.

4. Brush the salmon with a little of the glaze. Return the fish to the broiler for an additional 2 to 3 minutes.

Note: Cooking time depends on the thickness of the salmon. Watch closely to avoid overcooking the fish. In general, I remove the salmon just before I think it is done, because it will continue to cook once removed from the broiler.

5. Remove the salmon from the broiler and transfer to a serving dish. Cover the fish with the remaining glaze and serve with the brown rice.

Winter Week I: Tuesday

Winter Week 1: Wednesday

VEGETABLE MINESTRONE

Don't be fooled. This one-bowl meal is hearty enough to satisfy the whole family on a cold winter weeknight. I use Italian tomato paste and a Parmesan rind for rich, deep flavor. Ask for Parmesan rind at the cheese counter. Winter vegetables are roasted to bring out their sweet, nutty flavors. Make double and freeze for a handy weekend supper.

Serves 4: 35 minutes 

- 1 medium yellow onion, chopped
- 1 medium parsnip, peeled and chopped
- 2 medium carrots, peeled and chopped
- 2 celery stalks, sliced
- 2 medium zucchini, cubed, about ½ inch
- 2 medium yellow summer squash, cubed, about ½ inch
- 2 Tablespoons olive oil
- 1 teaspoon kosher salt
- ½ teaspoon ground cumin
- 8 cups low-sodium chicken or vegetable broth
- One 6-ounce can tomato paste
- 4 ounces Parmesan cheese, grated, plus a 3-inch Parmesan rind
- Two 14-ounce cans cannellini beans, drained and rinsed
- 4 ounces (1 cup) whole wheat farfalle (or other short pasta, like penne, ziti, or rigatoni)
- Black pepper to taste

1. Preheat the oven to 375°F.

2. Toss the vegetables with the olive oil, salt, and cumin and spread them on a large baking sheet. Roast for 25 minutes, until golden. Remove from the oven and let cool.

3. Meanwhile, combine the broth and tomato paste in a medium pot and bring to a simmer over medium heat. Add the Parmesan rind, the beans, and pasta and bring the liquid to a simmer again.

4. Add the vegetables to the broth and bring to a simmer. Season the soup with pepper to taste.

5. Serve the minestrone in individual serving bowls, garnished with the grated cheese.

GF omit pasta

 omit Parmesan

SPICY BEEF FARFALLE

Years ago, I ate a dish like this at a restaurant that has long since closed. But I still remember the layers of flavor derived from the rich beef, salty Parmesan, and fiery red chiles, and I just had to re-create that meal. This version is flexible and will work well without too much heat so the kids can enjoy it too. Thai chiles are small but pack a big punch. When in doubt, add a little at a time. Serve with a simple side of cucumber rounds to cool down the palate.

Serves 4: 20 minutes

- 1 Tablespoon olive oil
- ½ yellow onion, chopped
- 1 carrot, peeled and finely chopped
- 2 cups low-sodium chicken or vegetable broth
- 12 ounces whole wheat farfalle (or other short pasta, like penne, ziti, or rigatoni)
- ¼ teaspoon kosher salt
- ½ teaspoon black pepper
- 2 small fresh red Thai chile peppers, finely chopped, or to taste
- 1 pound leftover Crock-Pot Roast (see Monday, page 205), shredded (about 2 cups)
- ½ cup shredded Parmesan cheese
- 2 medium cucumbers, peeled and cut into rounds

1. Heat the olive oil in a medium skillet over medium heat. Add the onion and carrot and cook until the onion is soft and translucent, about 5 minutes.

2. Pour in the broth and bring to a simmer. Add the pasta and cook until the pasta has absorbed most of the liquid and is al dente, 8 to 10 minutes.

3. Season the pasta with the salt and pepper. Stir in the chile peppers. Fold in the beef and heat through.

4. Sprinkle the pasta with the Parmesan cheese before serving with the cucumber rounds alongside.

a fresh idea:

KIDS and SPICY FOOD

When it comes to adding heat in a dish, go slow; kids' taste buds can be sensitive. But a little spice doesn't hurt. Start with something mild, like a pinch of red pepper flakes, and always add a little at a time. Once the heat is in the dish, you can't take it back.

Winter Week 1: Thursday

Winter Week 1: Friday

FANCY FRANKS AND BEANS

This is everything a Friday night meal should be: simple and rib sticking. It takes a while to bake, but the hands-on time is minimal. Fresh sausage with fennel is my favorite for this dish. Dig in!

Serves 4–5: 1 hour  

- 1½ pounds chicken or Italian turkey sausage links
- 2 pints grape or cherry tomatoes
- 1 medium onion, thinly sliced
- 2 garlic cloves, minced or pressed
- 2 Tablespoons olive oil
- 1 Tablespoon balsamic vinegar
- 1 teaspoon dried oregano
- ½ teaspoon kosher salt
- ½ teaspoon black pepper
- 1 pound baby bok choy, roughly chopped
- Two 14-ounce cans cannellini beans (or great northern white beans), drained and rinsed

1. Preheat the oven to 375°F. Arrange the sausage in a 9-x-13-inch baking dish.

2. In a large bowl, toss together the tomatoes, onion, garlic, olive oil, vinegar, oregano, salt, and pepper. Pour the mixture over the sausages.

3. Bake for 30 minutes. Add the bok choy and beans to the casserole and stir to mix. Bake for 20 minutes, or until the casserole is slightly browned on top. Remove from the oven and let rest for 5 minutes before serving.

FAMILY FOOD CULTURE
Homegrown
the mccord family

Catherine McCord is deeply connected with food through her organic garden and love of local seasonal produce. A regular at the Sunday Hollywood Farmers' Market, she can often be seen scouring the stalls with her young family for the season's freshest produce. When she was growing up, her family food culture centered around well-being through diet, and Catherine now teaches her own children food respect and awareness.

Catherine has three simple rules to improve family eating:

1. Start early. The sooner children begin eating clean food bought close to the source, the better the chance they will adopt healthy choices.
2. Make it at home—better yet, grow it at home. By cooking your own meals, you can control the quality level of the food. Catherine grows fruits and vegetables all year round, and her kids know their way around her garden.
3. Kids are curious. The more you involve them, the more they will try new things and care about food.

mccord family food culture

SPECIAL OR RESTRICTED DIET: Organic, homegrown

WHO COOKS MOST MEALS?: Catherine and the kids

FAVORITE FAMILY MEAL: Breakfast

LEAST FAVORITE MEAL: Rushed takeout

STRICT RULE: Buy local

INDULGENCE: Cookies

BEST ADVICE FOR HEALTH: Be hands-on

HARDEST TREAT TO GIVE UP: Ice cream

ON THE NO-EAT LIST: Produce shipped internationally

WINTER MENU WEEK 2

MONDAY

Brick Chicken
with Collard Greens and Easy Scalloped Potatoes

TUESDAY

Chimichurri Fish
with Roasted Fennel and Potatoes

WEDNESDAY

Butternut Bisque
with Pear and Walnut Salad

THURSDAY

Arroz con Pollo
with Fennel and Peppers

FRIDAY

Croque Mama
with Marinated Collard Salad

SHOPPING LIST

Meat/Seafood

One 3½- to 4-pound chicken plus 1½ pounds boneless, skinless chicken thighs
1 pound thinly sliced lean Black Forest ham
1 pound tilapia fillets

Vegetables/Fruit

3 bunches collard greens
1 head red leaf lettuce
4 large russet potatoes (about 2 pounds)
¼ bunch fresh flat-leaf parsley
1 medium fennel bulb
1 red bell pepper
1 green bell pepper
1 medium sweet onion
2 medium butternut squash
4 Bosc pears
8 fresh sage leaves

Dairy

2 Tablespoons unsalted butter
1 cup 2% milk
6 ounces Gruyère cheese

Bakery/Misc.

¼ cup walnuts
1 whole wheat baguette

From the Pantry

4¾ teaspoons kosher salt
3½ teaspoons black pepper
1 teaspoon dried oregano
1½ teaspoons ground cumin
1¾ teaspoons sweet Hungarian paprika
2 teaspoons herbes de Provence
1 teaspoon red pepper flakes, plus a pinch
4 garlic cloves
3 Tablespoons grapeseed oil
1 cup plus 5 Tablespoons olive oil
Scant 7 Tablespoons white wine vinegar
1 Tablespoon balsamic vinegar
Scant 2 Tablespoons Dijon mustard
A heaping Tablespoon of tomato paste
7 to 8 cups low-sodium chicken or vegetable broth
2 cups brown rice (dry)
1½ Tablespoons The Fresh 20 Spice Blend (page xxii)

PREP AHEAD

Roasted Butternut Squash for Wednesday

2 medium butternut squash, cut lengthwise in half and seeds removed

1 Tablespoon olive oil

1. Preheat the oven to 425°F.

2. Arrange the squash flesh side up on a foil-lined baking sheet. Brush the squash with the olive oil.

3. Roast the squash for 45 minutes to 1 hour, until fork-tender. (For faster roasting, you can peel the squash, cut it into small cubes, place on the baking sheet, and roast for 25 minutes.)

4. Store the squash in an airtight container in the refrigerator for dinner on Wednesday.

cooking with kids

Part of The Fresh 20 philosophy is cooking together as a family. I understand many times it might be easier to leave kids out of the cooking process and just get dinner on the table. Make dinner prep part of quality time. Slow down. The more they are involved the more invested they are in eating well. Give them a responsibility that they can own.

A few ideas to keep (helpful) kids in the kitchen:

Measure ingredients

Pour liquids

Whisk dressings

Tear salad leaves

Cut soft vegetables and fruit with a dull kid's knife

Set table in fun patterns

PLC SPORTS DEPT.
CLASSIC
SUPERCHARGED Motors
IT'S GOOD!
HOME RUN!
GOAL

BRICK CHICKEN

with Collard Greens and Easy Scalloped Potatoes

When I married my husband, I knew I would have to perfect my roast chicken; it is his go-to dinner. Ten years later, my roast chicken is still a work in progress, but this grilled version satisfies my husband's cravings—in half the time! The skin comes out crisp and the meat is juicy. If you don't have a brick you can use a heavy cast-iron pot or skillet to weight the chicken. Start with the scalloped potatoes to time dinner perfectly.

Serves 4: 45 minutes 

for the brick chicken

One 3½- to 4-pound chicken, cut lengthwise in half

2 Tablespoons olive oil

1½ Tablespoons The Fresh 20 Spice Blend (page xxii)

for the collard greens

2 Tablespoons white wine vinegar

2 bunches collard greens, stems removed and cut into bite-sized pieces

1 teaspoon Dijon mustard

¼ teaspoon kosher salt

1 teaspoon black pepper

for the brick chicken

1. Preheat the oven to 375°F.
2. Brush the chicken with the olive oil. Rub the seasoning mix into the skin side of both halves of the chicken.
3. Heat a griddle or grill pan over high heat. Place the chicken skin side down on the griddle. Cover the chicken with aluminum foil. Wrap a clean brick in foil and carefully place it on top of the chicken to weight it down and flatten it. (You can also use a heavy cast-iron pot or skillet to weight down the chicken.) Sear for 7 to 10 minutes, until the chicken forms a golden-brown skin.
4. Remove the brick and flip the chicken. Place the pan in the oven and cook the chicken for 15 to 20 minutes or until the juices run clear when a thigh is pierced.

for the collard greens

1. Fill a large pot with water and bring to a boil. Add the vinegar and greens and cook for 20 minutes.
2. Drain and stir in the Dijon mustard, salt, and pepper.

for the easy scalloped potatoes

- 2 Tablespoons unsalted butter, plus more for the dish
- 2 large russet potatoes (about 1 pound), peeled and sliced into ⅛-inch slices
- 1 cup 2% milk
- 2 teaspoons herbes de Provence
- ½ teaspoon kosher salt
- ¼ teaspoon black pepper
- 2 ounces Gruyère cheese, grated (about ½ cup)

for the easy scalloped potatoes

1. Preheat the oven to 375°F. Lightly butter an 8-x-8-inch baking pan or small casserole dish.

2. Layer the potatoes evenly in the baking pan.

3. Combine the milk, butter, herbes de Provence, salt, and pepper in a small saucepan, and warm over low heat just until the butter melts.

4. Pour the milk over the potatoes and cover with foil. Carefully place the potatoes in the oven and bake for 25 to 30 minutes.

5. Remove the foil and top the potatoes with the cheese. Return the potatoes to the oven and cook, uncovered, for 10 minutes, or until the cheese is melted and the potatoes are cooked through.

Winter Week II: Monday

Winter Week II: Tuesday

a fresh idea:
SAUCES

Homemade sauces like pesto and chimichurri are perfect for freezing for emergency dinners. Toss with vegetables (peas, corn, zucchini) to make a quick side dish.

CHIMICHURRI FISH

with Roasted Fennel and Potatoes

Chimichurri is the dipping sauce served with bread in South American restaurants. I use the same blend to complement this fish. Chimichurri is wonderful to have on hand—make a double batch and use the extra as a vegetable dip or a pasta sauce.

Serves 4: 35 minutes  

for the chimichurri sauce

- ¼ cup finely chopped fresh flat-leaf parsley
- 2 garlic cloves, minced or pressed
- ½ cup olive oil
- ½ teaspoon kosher salt
- ¼ teaspoon black pepper
- 1 teaspoon red pepper flakes

for the fish

- 1 pound tilapia fillets
- ½ teaspoon kosher salt
- ¼ teaspoon black pepper
- ½ teaspoon sweet Hungarian paprika
- 1 Tablespoon grapeseed oil

for the roasted fennel and potatoes

- 2 large russet potatoes (about 1 pound), scrubbed and cut lengthwise into quarters and then into 1-inch cubes
- ½ medium fennel bulb, thinly sliced
- 3 Tablespoons olive oil
- ½ teaspoon kosher salt
- ¼ teaspoon black pepper

for the chimichurri sauce

Combine the parsley, garlic, olive oil, salt, black pepper, and red pepper flakes in an airtight container. Set aside. (The chimichurri can be refrigerated, tightly covered, for up to 3 days; bring to room temperature before serving.)

for the fish

1. Rinse the fish and pat dry with a paper towel. Sprinkle with the salt, pepper, and paprika on both sides.

2. Heat a large skillet over medium-high heat. Add the oil, and once it is hot, add the fish and cook for 2 to 3 minutes per side, or until the fish is golden brown and the flesh is opaque and slightly flaky.

3. Serve with the chimichurri.

for the roasted fennel and potatoes

1. Preheat the oven to 450°F.

2. Toss the potatoes and fennel together with the olive oil, salt, and pepper on a baking sheet, then spread out on the pan. Roast until the potatoes are golden brown and fork-tender, about 20 minutes.

BUTTERNUT BISQUE

with Pear and Walnut Salad

Roasting the squash brings out the natural sugars, which beautifully complement the sweet pears and the heady fragrance of the sage. This soul-satisfying soup is a staple of my winter kitchen; I always double the recipe.

Serves 4: 25 minutes   

for the butternut bisque

1 Tablespoon olive oil

¼ medium sweet onion, roughly chopped

2 Bosc pears, peeled, cut in half, and cored

8 fresh sage leaves, chopped

Roasted Butternut Squash (see Prep Ahead, page 218)

3 to 4 cups low-sodium chicken or vegetable broth

2 teaspoons white wine vinegar

½ teaspoon kosher salt

¼ teaspoon sweet Hungarian paprika

¼ teaspoon black pepper

for the pear and walnut salad

1 Tablespoon balsamic vinegar

3 Tablespoons olive oil

1 teaspoon Dijon mustard

Pinch each of kosher salt and black pepper

1 head red leaf lettuce, separated into leaves, washed, dried, and cut into bite-sized pieces

2 Bosc pears, cored and halved, each half cut lengthwise into 4 slices each

¼ cup walnuts, chopped

for the butternut bisque

1. Heat the oil in a medium pot over medium heat. Add the onion and pears, sprinkle with the sage, and sauté until softened, 3 to 4 minutes. Remove the pot from the heat.

2. Scoop the roasted squash from its skin. In batches, puree the squash with the onion, pears, and sage in a food processor. Add 3 cups of the broth a little at a time to the blender until the soup is creamy.

3. Return the pureed soup to the pot. Simmer the soup over low heat for an additional 10 minutes. Add some or all the additional broth as needed to reach a thick, creamy consistency. Season with the vinegar, salt, paprika, and pepper.

for the pear and walnut salad

1. In a small bowl, whisk together the vinegar, olive oil, Dijon, salt, and pepper.

2. In a medium salad bowl, combine the lettuce, pear slices, and walnuts. Toss with the dressing and serve.

Winter Week II: Wednesday

Winter Week II: Thursday

ARROZ CON POLLO
with Fennel and Peppers

Chicken and rice can be predictable, but fresh fennel gives this version an extra dimension. Using chicken thighs rather than breasts is both more economical and better tasting—the thighs don't dry out as easily in the oven.

Serves 5: 50 minutes  

for the chicken

- ½ teaspoon ground cumin
- 1 teaspoon sweet Hungarian paprika
- ½ teaspoon kosher salt
- ½ teaspoon black pepper
- 1½ pounds boneless, skinless chicken thighs
- 2 Tablespoons grapeseed oil

for the rice

- ½ medium sweet onion, thinly sliced
- ½ red bell pepper, thinly sliced
- ½ green bell pepper, thinly sliced
- ½ medium fennel bulb, cored and thinly sliced
- 1 Tablespoon olive oil
- 2 cups brown rice (dry)
- A heaping Tablespoon tomato paste
- 4 cups low-sodium chicken or vegetable stock
- 1 teaspoon dried oregano
- 1 teaspoon ground cumin
- 1 garlic clove, minced or pressed
- ½ teaspoon kosher salt
- ¼ teaspoon black pepper

for the chicken

1. In a small bowl, combine the cumin, paprika, salt, and pepper. Season the chicken thighs on both sides with the spice mix.

2. Heat the oil in a large deep skillet over medium heat. Once it is hot, add the chicken and sear until golden brown on both sides, about 3 minutes per side. Remove from the pan and set aside.

for the rice

1. Add the onion, bell peppers, and fennel to the pan, stir to combine, and cook until the vegetables begin to soften and the onions become translucent, about 3 minutes. Remove from the pan and set aside; set the pan aside.

2. Slice the chicken into bite-sized pieces; it is okay if it is still a little underdone, as it will finish cooking with the rice.

3. Add the olive oil to the skillet and heat over medium heat. Add the rice and stir to coat. Cook the rice, stirring, for 3 minutes, or until lightly browned. Add the tomato paste and stir to combine.

4. Add the chicken and vegetables to the skillet, pour in the broth, and stir to combine. Season with the oregano, cumin, garlic, salt, and pepper. Cover and bring to a boil, then reduce to a simmer and cook, covered, for 30 minutes.

CROQUE MAMA

with Marinated Collard Salad

Sometimes you just need a sandwich for dinner. This is my "mom" version of the French croque monsieur. I cut fat (and time) by omitting the traditional cream sauce for a healthier version. The slightly bitter taste of the raw collard greens complements the sweet ham and cheese. For best results, marinate the greens ahead of time.

Serves 4: 20 minutes

for the croque mama

1 whole wheat baguette

1 Tablespoon Dijon mustard

1 pound thinly sliced lean Black Forest ham

4 ounces Gruyère cheese, grated (about 1 cup)

for the marinated collard salad

2 Tablespoons olive oil

¼ cup white wine vinegar

1 garlic clove, minced or pressed

Pinch of red pepper flakes

1 teaspoon kosher salt

½ teaspoon black pepper

1 bunch collard greens, stems removed and trimmed, cut crosswise into thin ribbons

½ red bell pepper, thinly sliced

½ green bell pepper, thinly sliced

¼ medium sweet onion, thinly sliced

for the croque mama

1. Place a rack in the top third of the oven and preheat the oven to 425°F.

2. Slice the baguette lengthwise in half and cut each half into 6 equal pieces. Lightly spread some of the Dijon mustard on each piece, then top with 1 or 2 slices of ham and the cheese.

3. Place in the oven for 10 to 12 minutes, or until the bread has lightly browned and the cheese is melted and bubbly.

for the marinated collard salad

1. In a small bowl, whisk together the olive oil, vinegar, garlic, red pepper flakes, salt, and pepper.

2. In a large bowl, combine the collard greens, bell peppers, and onion with the dressing and then, with your hands, gently massage the dressing into the collards to wilt them. Chill until ready to serve.

Winter Week II: Friday

WINTER MENU

WEEK 3

MONDAY
Turkey Chili

TUESDAY
Shrimp and Grits

WEDNESDAY
French Onion Soup
with Caesar Salad

THURSDAY
Turkey Meatballs
with Gravy and Brussels Sprouts

FRIDAY
Winter Steak
with Caramelized Onions
and Garlic Mushrooms

SHOPPING LIST

Meat/Seafood

2½ pounds lean ground turkey
1 pound medium shrimp
1¼ to 1½ pounds boneless New York steak (2 steaks)

Vegetables/Fruit

1 head romaine lettuce
6 large onions
1 small bunch fresh thyme
1 Tablespoon fresh flat-leaf parsley
1 pound Roma tomatoes (hothouse)
1 bell pepper
2 poblano chile peppers
12 ounces plus 6 whole mushrooms (button or cremini)
1 lemon
½ pound Brussels sprouts

Dairy

1 large egg
3 cups 2% milk
4 Tablespoons unsalted butter
1¾ cups Parmesan

Bakery/Misc.

Two 15-ounce cans cannellini beans (can substitute any bean)
1 cup yellow medium-coarse cornmeal (grits)
1 cup white wine
1 whole wheat baguette

From the Pantry

6 Tablespoons olive oil
3 Tablespoons grapeseed oil
10 garlic cloves
5 teaspoons kosher salt
3¼ teaspoons black pepper
½ teaspoon cayenne pepper
½ teaspoon dried oregano
½ teaspoon ground cumin
1 Tablespoon herbes de Provence
12 cups low-sodium chicken or vegetable broth
3 Tablespoons whole wheat flour
¼ cup homemade mayonnaise (page 27)

a fresh idea:

LET THERE BE MUSIC!

Take turns at playing DJ and put on some music while cooking. Music improves moods, relaxes everyone, and adds joy to most any situation.

My kitchen music list:

- Aretha Franklin
- John Mayer
- Amy Winehouse
- Earth, Wind, and Fire
- Gypsy Kings

PREP AHEAD

Caramelized Onions for Wednesday and Friday

2 Tablespoons olive oil

4½ large onions, thinly sliced

1. Heat the oil in a 5-quart Dutch oven over medium heat. Add the onions and cook, stirring occasionally, until they soften and start to brown, at least 30 minutes.

2. Store the onions in an airtight container in the refrigerator for up to 5 days.

Yield: 4 cups

Meatballs for Thursday

One 2-inch slice of whole wheat baguette, cut into cubes

½ cup low-sodium chicken or vegetable broth

¼ medium yellow onion, finely chopped

1¼ pounds lean ground turkey

1 large egg yolk

6 button or cremini mushrooms, wiped clean and minced

1 teaspoon kosher salt

½ teaspoon black pepper

1 Tablespoon finely chopped fresh flat-leaf parsley

1. Place the baguette cubes in a small bowl. Pour the broth over them and set aside to soak.

2. In a large bowl, combine the onion, ground turkey, egg yolk, mushrooms, salt, pepper, and parsley. Use your hands to really mix it up! Add the soggy bread to the turkey mix and mix well.

3. With wet hands, form the meat mixture into 1-inch meatballs; you should have 20 to 24. Store the meatballs in a Ziploc bag, laid flat, in the refrigerator for up to 4 days.

Winter Week III: Monday

TURKEY CHILI

Every family should have a go-to meal. This is mine. Quick to prepare and easy to save and reheat as leftovers. My sister, Kristen, is the turkey chili expert and makes a similar version for impromptu winter gatherings with friends.

Serves 6: 25 minutes  

- 2 Tablespoons grapeseed oil
- 1 medium yellow onion, diced
- 1 garlic clove, minced or pressed
- 1 poblano chile pepper, seeds removed and finely chopped
- 1¼ pounds lean ground turkey
- 1 teaspoon kosher salt
- ½ teaspoon ground cumin
- ½ teaspoon dried oregano
- ½ teaspoon black pepper
- ¼ teaspoon cayenne pepper (optional)
- 1 pound Roma tomatoes (hothouse), chopped
- 4 cups low-sodium chicken or vegetable broth
- 2 cups water
- Two 15-ounce cans cannellini beans (can substitute any bean), drained and rinsed

1. Heat the oil in a medium pot over medium-high heat. Add the onion and sauté for 3 minutes, until translucent. Add the garlic and poblano pepper and sauté for 3 to 4 minutes.

2. Mix in the meat and brown until it is no longer pink. Season with the salt, cumin, oregano, black pepper, and optional cayenne pepper.

3. Add the tomatoes, broth, and water and bring to a simmer. Add the beans and bring to a boil, then the reduce heat to low. Cover the pot and simmer for 8 to 10 minutes.

SHRIMP AND GRITS

It's true, grits need the attention of a frequent stir, but they cook quickly. Avoid fine cornmeal or polenta and opt for a medium-course variety. Bob's Red Mill (see Resources) has a good selection of yellow cornmeal.

Serves 4: 25 minutes 

for the grits

2 cups water

2 cups 2% milk

1 cup yellow medium-coarse cornmeal (grits)

½ teaspoon kosher salt

1 Tablespoon unsalted butter

1 Tablespoon thyme leaves

½ cup grated Parmesan cheese

for the shrimp

2 Tablespoons olive oil

1 garlic clove, minced or pressed

1 bell pepper, cored, seeded, and chopped

1 poblano chile pepper, seeded and chopped

½ teaspoon kosher salt

¼ teaspoon cayenne pepper

¼ teaspoon black pepper

1 pound medium shrimp, peeled and deveined

for the grits

1. In a large saucepan, bring the water and milk to a simmer over medium heat. Slowly add the grits, stirring to prevent clumps. Cook, stirring frequently, until the liquid has been absorbed, about 15 minutes.

2. Fold in the salt, butter, thyme, and Parmesan.

for the shrimp

1. In a large skillet, heat the olive oil over high heat. Add the garlic, bell pepper, and poblano chile and sauté until tender. Season with the salt, cayenne, and black pepper.

2. Toss in the shrimp and cook, stirring frequently, for 5 minutes.

3. Serve the shrimp over the grits.

Winter Week III:
Tuesday

Winter Week III: Wednesday

FRENCH ONION SOUP

with Caesar Salad

This soup requires patience. While it is easy to cook, and requires limited prep time, you'll need to stay close to the kitchen to watch the onions as they sweat it out over a medium flame. The payoff is a sweet, savory broth that makes you feel as if all is right in the world.

Serves 4: 35 minutes 

for the french onion soup

3 cups Caramelized Onions (see Prep Ahead, page 233)

2 garlic cloves, minced or pressed

4 fresh thyme sprigs

½ teaspoon kosher salt

2 Tablespoons whole wheat flour

1 cup white wine

6 cups low-sodium chicken or vegetable broth

2 cups water

8 slices whole wheat baguette, toasted

1 cup shredded Parmesan cheese

1 teaspoon black pepper

for the caesar salad

¼ cup mayonnaise, homemade (page 27)

2 garlic cloves, minced or pressed

Juice of 1 lemon

¼ teaspoon kosher salt

½ teaspoon black pepper

2 Tablespoons olive oil

¼ cup grated Parmesan cheese

1 head romaine lettuce, washed, dried, and chopped

for the french onion soup

1. Combine the onions, garlic, thyme, and salt in a large Dutch oven and cook on medium until the garlic is fragrant.

2. Mix in the flour and cook for 2 minutes, or until it no longer smells like raw flour. Stir in the white wine, broth, and water. Partially cover the pot, bring to a simmer, and simmer until the flavors are well blended, about 20 minutes. Meanwhile, preheat the broiler.

3. Arrange the toast on top of the soup and sprinkle with the cheese and pepper. Put under the broiler for 10 minutes, or until the cheese bubbles and is slightly browned.

4. Divide the soup among deep serving bowls. Serve with the salad.

for the caesar salad

1. In a small bowl, whisk together the mayonnaise, garlic, lemon juice, salt, pepper, olive oil, and Parmesan. Chill the dressing.

2. In a medium salad bowl, toss the romaine with the dressing.

DIY *chicken broth*

Making your own broth is not only satisfying, it's easy. A few basic ingredients, water, and time are all you need to enhance your weeknight cooking with fresh broth.

Broth freezes well in 2-cup portions for quick weeknight additions.

- 1 Tablespoon olive oil
- 1 medium onion, coarsely chopped
- 3 medium carrots, coarsely chopped
- 2 medium celery stalks, coarsely chopped
- One 3½- to 4-pound chicken
- 8 cups water
- 1 teaspoon kosher salt

1. In a large stockpot, heat the oil over medium-high heat. Once the oil sizzles, add the onion, carrots, and celery and sauté for about 5 minutes, until the edges start to brown.

2. Add the chicken and water, bring to a simmer, and cover. Cook for 45 minutes to 1 hour, skimming any foam and fat off the top. Remove the chicken from the broth and let cool; leave the broth at a simmer.

3. When the chicken is cool, remove the meat from the bones and store in an airtight container in the refrigerator or freezer to use in another meal. Add the bones back to the broth.

4. Add the salt to the broth and continue to simmer for 30 more minutes.

5. Strain the broth through cheesecloth or a fine-mesh strainer; discard the solids. Let cool.

6. Store the broth in 2-cup portions; Ziploc bags are nice because you can store them flat in the freezer.

Tips

- Skim the fat off the top while the broth simmers.
- Use any leftover chicken to make a small batch of broth.
- Shred the chicken meat and freeze for quick meals in a pinch.

Add-ins

- Any curry powder or fragrant spice will add a new dynamic to the broth. Try a tablespoon of something exotic.
- Make it vegetarian! Eliminate the chicken and double the vegetables.

Serving Ideas

- In Japan, broth is served at breakfast. Try a warm bowl before starting your day.
- Keep a few cups in the freezer for a quick and easy soup on hectic weeknights. Just add vegetables and bring to a boil and you'll have a deliciously simple soup.
- Cooking grains like brown rice and quinoa in broth gives them a more complex flavor profile and can improve the overall taste of your meal.

TURKEY MEATBALLS

with Gravy and Brussels Sprouts

These meatballs are hands down the most requested The Fresh 20 dinner. They are best when made a few days ahead of time. The pan gravy is simple to master. Don't skip the fresh parsley; it adds a subtle flavor. Any green vegetable works well as a side dish for this meal, but my preference is Brussels sprouts.

Serves 4: 25 minutes

for the turkey meatballs

½ cup low-sodium chicken or vegetable broth

Meatballs (see Prep Ahead, page 233)

for the gravy

1 Tablespoon unsalted butter

1 Tablespoon whole wheat flour

1 cup low-sodium chicken or vegetable broth

1 cup 2% milk

for the brussels sprouts

1 Tablespoon unsalted butter

2 garlic cloves

½ pound Brussels sprouts, rinsed and cut in half

¼ teaspoon kosher salt

1 Tablespoon water

for the turkey meatballs

Heat the broth in a large skillet over medium heat. Add the meatballs and cook for 10 minutes, turning frequently, until the liquid is absorbed and the meatballs are browned on all sides. Transfer the meatballs to a plate lined with paper towels.

for the gravy

1. Increase the heat to high, add the butter, and stir up the bits of browned meatballs left in the pan. Whisk in the flour and cook, whisking, until the mixture is slightly browned and the raw flour smell has disappeared, about 2 minutes. Whisk in the broth and reduce the heat to medium-low. Whisk in the milk and cook, stirring, until the gravy thickens.

2. Add the meatballs to the pan and simmer for 5 minutes, stirring frequently.

for the brussels sprouts

1. Melt the butter and garlic in a sauté pan over medium-high heat.

2. Add the Brussels sprouts and cook until edges start to turn golden brown.

3. Sprinkle with the salt. Add the water. Cover and cook for 5 minutes.

Winter Week III: Thursday

Winter Week III: Friday

WINTER STEAK

with Caramelized Onions and Garlic Mushrooms

Just because the grill might be covered by snow doesn't mean you can't enjoy a perfectly charred grilled steak. Take it to the grill pan! A cast-iron skillet works nicely as well.

Serves 4: 20 minutes 

for the steak

1¼ to 1½ pounds boneless New York steak (2 steaks)

1 Tablespoon grapeseed oil

¾ teaspoon kosher salt

½ teaspoon black pepper

1 Tablespoon herbes de Provence

1 cup Caramelized Onions (see Prep Ahead, page 233)

for the garlic mushrooms

2 garlic cloves, minced or pressed

1 Tablespoon unsalted butter

12 ounces button or cremini mushrooms, sliced

⅛ teaspoon kosher salt

Dash of black pepper

Leftover Brussels sprouts (see Thursday, page 242)

for the steak

1. Remove the steaks from the refrigerator about 20 minutes before cooking; this will allow the steaks to cook more evenly. Brush a grill pan with the oil and heat over high heat. Season the steaks with the salt, pepper, and herbes de Provence on both sides.
2. Place the steaks on the grill pan and cook for 3 to 4 minutes per side, without moving them, or until the desired doneness is achieved. This timing is for medium for 1-inch-thick steaks; adjust the cooking time accordingly. Remove from the pan and allow the steaks to rest for 5 minutes before slicing.
3. Meanwhile, heat the caramelized onions in a small saucepan.
4. Serve the onions over the steak.

for the garlic mushrooms

1. Sauté the garlic in butter over medium heat until fragrant.
2. Add the mushrooms. Stir to coat.
3. Cook 3 to 4 minutes, until softened.
4. Sprinkle with salt and pepper. Serve warm.
5. Serve with leftover Brussels sprouts.

WINTER MENU

MONDAY

Pork Verde
with Parsley Quinoa

TUESDAY

Mussels in Brodo
with Roasted Parsley-Butter Cauliflower

WEDNESDAY

Cabbage-Pork Stew

THURSDAY

Mushroom Polenta

FRIDAY

Citrus Chicken
with Quinoa Salad

SHOPPING LIST

Meat/Seafood

2 pounds pork tenderloins
1 pound organic chicken breast (about 2)
2 pounds mussels

Vegetables/Fruit

1 large bunch fresh flat-leaf parsley (1½ cups)
2 medium onions
2 pounds green tomatillos
1 poblano chile pepper
1 jalapeño pepper
2 lemons
1 lime
1 small head cauliflower
1 head green cabbage
2 shallots
½ ounce dried porcini mushrooms
2 cups frozen corn

Dairy

5 Tablespoons unsalted butter
½ cup grated Parmesan

Bakery/Misc.

2½ cups quinoa (dry)
1 cup white wine
1 cup fine cornmeal (polenta)

From the Pantry

8 Tablespoons olive oil
8 garlic cloves
3½ teaspoons kosher salt
1¼ teaspoon black pepper
¼ teaspoon cayenne pepper
1 teaspoon sweet Hungarian paprika
4 Tablespoons tomato paste
8 cups low-sodium chicken or vegetable broth

PREP AHEAD

Quinoa for Monday and Friday

Prepare 6 cups quinoa (see page xvii).

Tomatillos for Monday

Prep tomatillos by removing the paperlike wrapper and rinsing in warm water to remove any sticky residue

Poblano for Monday

Remove seeds and cut into quarters

picky eaters

Start with simple ingredients and work toward more complex, multi-ingredient meals. Never assume your child will dislike a particular food: serve new foods enthusiastically, and don't get discouraged. The most common mistake I see parents make in the war on picky eaters is giving up and giving in. Resist the urge to make an alternative: serve one dinner with reasonable adjustments. And never accept defeat: continue to serve the offending items in various forms and recipes. It can take up to ten times before someone develops a taste for an ingredient.

Picky Eater Survival Tips:

- Involve picky eaters in kitchen prep, and make it fun.
- Be creative with presentation—serve broccoli in a teacup.
- Assign a grocery task: pick a certain color of fruit, pick out a vegetable to try.
- Start small so it doesn't seem like an insurmountable portion.
- Be flexible but stern—you don't have to be a short-order cook.

Winter Week IV:
Monday

PORK VERDE

with Parsley Quinoa

There are red salsa lovers like me and then there are green salsa lovers like everyone else in my house. When tomatillos are available, I make a large batch of "verde" to use as salsa, sauce, and stew. These green "tomatoes" pack a unique flavor.

Serves 4–6: 45 minutes  

for the pork verde

2 pounds pork tenderloins

½ teaspoon kosher salt

½ teaspoon black pepper

2 Tablespoons olive oil

1 medium onion, coarsely chopped

2 garlic cloves, cut in half

2 pounds green tomatillos, husked, rinsed, and cut in half

1 poblano chile pepper, seeded and quartered

½ jalapeño pepper, seeded and quartered

Juice of 1 lime

2 cups low-sodium chicken or vegetable broth

for the parsley quinoa

3 cups prepared quinoa

½ cup chopped fresh flat-leaf parsley

¼ teaspoon cayenne pepper

½ teaspoon kosher salt

Juice of ½ lemon

for the pork verde

1. Rub the pork tenderloins with the salt and pepper.
2. Heat the olive oil in a 5-quart saucepan over medium-high heat.
3. Arrange the pork in the pan and brown on all sides, about 10 minutes total. Remove the pork and set aside.
4. Add the onion, garlic, tomatillos, poblano chile, jalapeño, and lime juice to the pan and sauté until soft, about 10 minutes.
5. Place the browned pork tenderloin on top of the vegetables. Add the broth.
6. Cover and let simmer for 10 minutes. Transfer the meat to a serving dish and cover in foil to rest for 5 minutes.
7. Blend the tomatillo mixture with an immersion or regular blender until smooth.
8. Slice half of the meat and arrange it on a platter over quinoa. Cover with 2 cups of tomatillo sauce.

Leftover Note: Reserve the other half of the meat and at least 1 cup of the sauce for dinner on Wednesday.

for the parsley quinoa

Combine quinoa with parsley, cayenne, salt, and lemon juice in a medium serving bowl. Chill until ready to serve.

MUSSELS IN BRODO

with Roasted Parsley-Butter Cauliflower

To be honest, I was never really a fan of mussels, so I wanted to create a recipe delicious enough to convert me. This does the trick, with a garlicky aroma and savory wine undertones. A sprinkle of fresh parsley enhances the flavor even more.

Serves 4: 35 minutes 

for the roasted cauliflower

3 Tablespoons unsalted butter

2 Tablespoons olive oil

1 small head cauliflower, quartered

¼ cup chopped fresh flat-leaf parsley

½ teaspoon salt

for the mussels

1 cup low-sodium chicken or vegetable broth

4 garlic cloves, minced or pressed

1 cup white wine

Juice of ½ lemon

½ teaspoon kosher salt

2 pounds mussels

½ cup fresh flat-leaf parsley leaves

for the roasted cauliflower

1. Preheat the oven to 375°F.

2. Melt the butter with the oil in a small saucepan.

3. On a baking sheet, toss the cauliflower with the melted butter and oil. Spread out on the pan, sprinkle the cauliflower with the parsley and salt, and bake for 30 minutes, or until golden brown.

for the mussels

1. Bring the broth to a simmer in a large pot over low heat. Stir in the garlic, white wine, lemon juice, and salt.

2. Arrange the mussels in the pot and top with the parsley. Cover and steam the mussels for 3 to 5 minutes, until they open fully. Discard any mussels that don't open.

Winter Week IV: Tuesday

Winter Week IV: Wednesday

CABBAGE-PORK STEW

This stew happened one night when there was only enough leftover meat for one person but four hungry mouths. Making the most of the situation required adding some vegetables and broth and bringing everything up to a simmer. Stew happens. Now I make this dish even when there are no leftovers around.

Serves 5: 15 minutes  

2 Tablespoons olive oil

1 head green cabbage, core removed and chopped

1 cup frozen corn

¼ cup tomato paste

2 cups low-sodium chicken or vegetable broth

½ teaspoon sweet Hungarian paprika

About 1¾ pound leftover Pork Verde, plus sauce (see Monday, page 251), cut into pieces

Salt and black pepper to taste

1. Heat the olive oil in a 5-quart Dutch oven or other heavy pot over medium heat. Add the cabbage and corn and sauté for 5 minutes.

2. Add the tomato paste, stirring to coat.

3. Pour in the broth and bring to a simmer. Add the paprika and pork verde, with the sauce, and simmer until the meat is heated through.

4. Season with salt and black pepper to taste.

MUSHROOM POLENTA

Dried corn has many personalities. When cracked and ground into a fine meal, corn is called polenta. It's the same as grits, but with a finer texture. Here the polenta takes center stage, accompanied by dried mushrooms that add layers of flavor. The basics of making a batch of polenta never change, but the mix-in options are endless. In the morning, polenta with maple syrup and blueberries gives tired pancakes a break. Once the technique is solid, let the experimentation begin!

Serves 4: 35 minutes  

½ ounce dried porcini mushrooms

1 cup warm water

2 Tablespoons unsalted butter

2 shallots, minced

2 garlic cloves, minced or pressed

3 cups low-sodium chicken or vegetable broth

1 cup fine cornmeal (polenta)

1 teaspoon kosher salt

½ teaspoon black pepper

½ cup grated Parmesan

1. Soak the porcini mushrooms in warm water for 20 minutes. Drain the mushrooms and reserve the water.

2. In a Dutch oven, melt the butter over medium heat. Sauté the shallots and garlic until translucent.

3. Add the broth and mushroom water; bring to boil.

4. Whisk in the corn meal until well blended.

5. Simmer, stirring frequently, for 25 minutes, until soft and thick.

6. Stir in the salt, pepper, mushrooms, and cheese.

7. Remove from heat and serve immediately.

Winter Week IV: Thursday

Winter Week IV: Friday

CITRUS CHICKEN

with Quinoa Salad

At the end of a busy week, I look to what's quick and convenient. Quinoa always delivers. Versatile, simple to prepare, and packed with protein, it has become a staple. This recipe gives you the basic building blocks of a grain salad: an aromatic (onion), a protein, a vegetable, and a fresh herb. The possibilities are endless and as the last recipe in the book, I invite you to get creative with dinner.

Serves 4: 20 minutes  

- 2 Tablespoons olive oil
- 1 medium onion, chopped
- ½ jalapeño pepper, seeded and diced
- ½ teaspoon paprika
- ½ teaspoon kosher salt
- ¼ teaspoon black pepper
- 2 chicken breasts, cut into bite-sized cubes
- 1 cup frozen corn
- ¼ cup fresh flat-leaf parsley
- 3 cups prepared quinoa
- 1 lemon, cut into 8 wedges

1. In a 5-quart saucepan, heat the olive oil over medium heat. Add the onion and jalapeño and cook until translucent, about 5 minutes.

2. Stir in the paprika, salt, and pepper until combined.

3. Add the chicken and cook for 10 minutes, until no longer pink.

4. Toss in the corn, parsley, and quinoa. Stir to combine.

5. Serve with the lemon wedges.

A FINAL NOTE

I realize a family food culture can shift over the years, but ultimately, it is always about bringing the family to the table one way or another. This book is for home cooks and I hope after reading it that you feel better equipped with the tools, tips, skills, and information needed to achieve success in the kitchen—however you define that—on even the busiest of weeknights. How lucky we are to live at a time when fresh food is celebrated and so many understand the connection between eating well and feeling good. My food habits have been decades in the making. Today I feel so fortunate that my life led me to health and happiness.

There is much more to say about food, and I have only scratched the surface. If you would like to continue the conversation, please visit me at www.thefresh20.com.

to your wild kitchen success!

Delish
COOKING SCHOOL
Bittman
How to Cook Everything
the basics
CookingLight
Krieger
comfort food fix
SWANSON
super natural every day
Mark Bittman
THE FOOD MATTERS COOKBOOK
THE FAMILY DINNER
Great Ways to CONNECT with Your Kids, One Meal at a Time
LAURIE DAVID

Some of my favorite home-cooking resources . . .

Books

Cooking Light: Way to Cook Light

I love everything about this resourceful book. Great images, simple instructions, and organized for real kitchen use. One of the most used in my collection.

How to Cook Everything by Mark Bittman

I love this entire series for being nothing but utile and easy on beginner cooks.

Comfort Food Fix by Elie Krieger

I adore the lovely Elie Krieger. She has such an accessible tone in her recipes and this book lightens up those heavy old comfort favorites families love so much.

Almost Meatless by Joy Manning

This book has some wonderful recipes using meat as an accent. A delicious book for anyone looking to reduce meat consumption.

Delish Cooking School by the editors of Delish

If you are a visual person, this book will delight your eyes with step-by-step pictures on the basics of cooking. A great resource for the home cook and one of my favorites.

Websites

www.kidshealth.org

www.eatingrules.com

www.100daysofrealfood.com

Online Retailers

Melissa's Produce www.melissaproduce.com

Melissa's distributes over 1,700 different types of produce. I'm a big fan and they have supported The Fresh 20 from very early on. Most of the produce we chopped, cooked, photographed, and tested for this cookbook was generously donated by Melissa's. And I like their name, too.

Bob's Red Mill www.bobsredmill.com

A leader in grains, cereal, and beans, Bob's Red Mill is my go-to solution for The Fresh 20 pantry. Look for cornmeal/polenta, couscous, farro, and beans.

Penzey's Spices www.penzeys.com

I've used this mail-order company for more than a decade. Good variety. Consistent quality.

Equipment

This is what you will find in my kitchen. I look for the best-quality tools I can afford.

Le Creuset (worth the splurge) www.lecreuset.com

All-Clad (lasts a lifetime) www.all-clad.com

Analon (favorite nonstick) www.analon.com

Kitchen Aid (a reliable friend) www.kitchenaid.com

Vitamix (powerhouse blender) www.vitamix.com

First and foremost, I'd like to thank my editor, Amy Bendell, who turned a thirty-two-minute conversation between strangers into a 320-page project between friends. I will always be grateful.

The entire team at HarperCollins for taking me in and believing I could accomplish the death-defying feat of authorship.

This book was made possible in large part by Louise Mellor, who styled every photo and made suggestions in every area. My sincere gratitude for keeping it moving forward and being part of our Tuesdays.

To my publicist, Nicole Kalish, who put all her faith in The Fresh 20 and made this a team effort. Thank goodness for the unsinkable Molly O'Neill, who guided me right on past the rough spots and confirmed the author was inside me.

A special thank-you to everyone who opened their doors to me and let me into their family food culture. I'm talking to you, Aherns, McCords, and Andersons.

To my sister, Kristen, who has always been there for me along the journey. To Bill, for believing. To Alan, whose strong and silent love took great care of Eileen.

To Sellers and Anderson, my lifelong friends who unconditionally love me and hold me up when I can't do it myself.

To my Baker crew, who taught me how to cook, especially Marty, who drove to the store when a little girl didn't want to stop baking.

To the Osman clan for keeping me safe in Eileen's absence.

To all the families who have shared my kitchen table and lingered over friendship. God bless the Anderson, Bellamy, Blincoe, Bolden, Bugh, Butler, Chong, DiOrio, Fisher, Heymann, Jacobs, Lanz, Limerick, Marsh, McKewon, and Sellers families.

To The Fresh 20 kids: Bailey, Baron, Hannah, Tatum, Maxx, Paris, Quinn, Luc, Maison, Alton, Savanna—You are the future. Eat your peas.

To Bob and Diane, for reminding me that nothing is more important than breaking bread with your family.

To Christina for her constant support and boundless energy, Te quiero.

My **Trent**. You are my emotional, physical pantry and you are never empty. Every day more I love you. Thank you for loving me in a deep and profound way with patience, encouragement, and pride.

More than anything, I want to thank my boys, **Aiden and Eliott**, for telling Mommy she was writing the best cookbook ever and always providing extra kisses when needed.

Recipe Testers

To the army of subscribers who diligently tested the recipes within this book, I thank you.

Amanda Abbott, Tracy Arbaugh, Shana Cook, Dawn Copple, Judy Garris, Elizabeth Graham, Heather Hampton, Erin Holley, Cathy Hunter, Chrissy Kinney, Amy Knudsen, Emily Kuhn, Charlotte Lee, Chelle Leininger, Natasha Matieschyn, Kristeen Mendoza, Sarah Nance, Erin Perrigo, Laura Rawson, Shannon Smith, Lindsey Swank-Meili, Cheryl Thompson, Allie Tiedeman, Dottie Wieclawska, Holly Wunker.

May you all find happiness in your kitchen.

Note: Page numbers in *italics* refer to illustrations.

A

B

C

D

E

F

G

H

N

O

P

Q

R

S

T

V

W

Y

Z